THIS BOOK MUST BE RETURNED OR RENEWED
ON OR BEFORE THE LAST DATE SHOWN BELOW

VISIT OUR WEBSITE www.iow.gov.uk/thelibrary
(Borrower and PIN number required for both services)

ISLE OF WIGHT LIBRARIES

09. NOV 21

19. APR 22

18. JUN 24

Published by thefluidway©

ISBN 978-1-8380210-2-3

**Cover Design Ligeia Vagharshagian
Cover photo Pixabay CC0**
https://pixabay.com/illustrations/smiley-emoji-emote-symbol-emoticon-1041796/

To contact the author
https://thefluidway.com/contact-us/

Disclaimer

This book is not intended to provide medical advice or to take the place of medical advice and treatment from your personal physician. Readers must consult qualified health professionals regarding the treatment of any medical problems. The author does not take any responsibility for any possible consequences from any action or application to any person reading or following the information in this book.

Website information is correct at the time of publishing. However, no liability can be accepted for any information or links found on third-party websites which are subject to change.

Unless otherwise indicated, Bible quotations are taken from the New King James version of the Bible

CONTENTS

THE BOLD CLAIM

The Fruit of the Spirit is the way to whole and happy living. That's quite a claim to make. So, can I back that up in life, in the real world? Yes! In this book we will be exploring the incredible ways the Spirit of God enables us to grow to make sure that we can enjoy a whole and happy life. The result? No matter what you face in life, you will have the emotional and mental empowerment to not only survive but thrive. Together, we will also explore happiness: what it is and why God wants you to live a life in true happiness, and how you can.

By taking an in-depth look at the Fruit and the healing and liberating power locked in the Fruit and in each manifestation of the Fruit, we will discover how to access this in our own lives to bring about whole living. This is about living in the fullness of the Fruit, just as God intended so that your life is whole on all levels.

The Holy Spirit was given specifically by God to empower every believer to live a life of kingdom destiny. The Gifts of the Spirit found in 1 Corinthians 12 were given to empower us in our daily kingdom living. **These Gifts work Spirit to spirit. The Holy Spirit works through our renewed**

spirits to channel the power of God and eternal heaven through us as a declaration of the love and presence of God.

Having the power of heaven at our disposal carries a responsibility with it. **The gift of the Holy Spirit was given so that we may learn through Him how to live in the kingdom in preparation for our eternal future in the presence of God and in eternal heaven.** That means each of us has to develop within the possibility and power given, find how we fit into God's great plan and develop ourselves to fill that place in this world and the next. We are developing so that we can reign and rule with Christ effectively, and that means we have to develop in each area of life.

This is the reason for the Fruit of the Spirit. **The Fruit works Spirit to mind. The Fruit enables us to operate within the limitless power and ability of the Gifts in wholeness and balance.** It flows through the nine manifestations mentioned in Galatians 5:22, impacting every area of life. It is the undergirding and compelling force behind the effective operation of the Gifts ensuring the Gifts may flow from a point of wholeness within you.

Let's look at an example. If you're given the fictitious superpower of heat vision, you would have to explore the range of the gift in controlled surroundings to understand the scope of what you can do. You'd also have to learn to control yourself so that you use your superpower in thoughtful, productive and constructive ways. You don't want to unleash your heat vision on some unsuspecting bystander!

Although the safeguard of the Gifts is that the Spirit releases the Gifts as He wills, our intent and will still features in the equation. Most of us have experienced the 'word' given or the prophecy offered that comes from a hidden agenda or a broken place in the giver. The Gifts flow through mature and immature alike and is not a measure of the person. The Spirit's intention is that we would co-operate to hone ourselves and the Gifts He entrusts us with, by operating His Gifts from a place of wholeness. That's our part.

The Spirit offers you the power of the Gifts and the wholeness of the Fruit. **The Gifts work Spirit to spirit, given as the Spirit wills. The Fruit works Spirit to mind and unlike the Gifts, we use our minds and wills to grow in the Fruit.** You reveal this in your own life and it releases the blessings of kingdom living and the result is: John 14:12-14 "Most assuredly, I say to you, he who believes in Me, the works that I do he will do also; and greater works than these he will do, because I go to My Father. And whatever you ask in My name, that I will do, that the Father may be glorified in the Son. If you ask anything in My name, I will do it."

The Fruit of the Spirit enables you to think and act like God in your use of kingdom power and works Spirit to mind.

In exploring the Gifts, we find only half the story of what we've been given. **In order to fully operate in the Holy Spirit and be fully ready for all the amazing Gifts to flow through us we need the character of God so we can function in power as God does.** We need the Fruit of the Spirit. The power of the nine Gifts finds exquisite and perfect balance in the wholeness the Fruit continuously produces.

The Fruit was given as healing to the damage the marring effect that wrong thinking has on our mental realm: our emotions, our will, our intellect, our imagination and our memory and the way the damage in the mental realm changes our perception and the way we respond to God, life and others. In order to reign in this life and the next effectively, we need to embrace the healing offered and co-operate with the Spirit to make this healing happen.

Just as the gift of tongues, for example, doesn't change the language we speak or our way of speaking, the manifestation of the Fruit doesn't change the fact that we were marred by wrong thinking. However, just as we unite in God's purpose in speaking the unified purpose of the Spirit language of tongues, so the manifestation of the Fruit brings a point of wholeness through which we can create new thinking and live destiny as if we had never been marred. **We can actually remake our minds and emotions so that we think and live in the same potential in which Jesus lived.**

Imagine that. Living without the damaging effects of wrong thinking and wrongdoing, with limitless possibilities offered in the kingdom of God! We are going to explore the incredible range of living in all that has been given to believers and how we access the full potential of all we have throughout the book.

The whole Fruit.

The nine manifestations of the Fruit of the Spirit are grounded in the love that is God. Note that Fruit is singular. Love, joy, peace etc. are not the fruits of the Spirit but the manifestation or evidence of the Fruit of the Spirit. It's a complete and whole package. Imagine a cluster of grapes being one cluster but having many grapes on the cluster. Each grape has the full taste of 'grape-iness' contained in itself – the cluster in miniature. The manifestation of the Fruit is the same. Fruit is the entire cluster, while love, joy, peace etc. are the individual grapes on the one cluster, that combined, form the healing of the Fruit.

These manifestations blend together to create the perfect blueprint of how to think with a new mind and live in a whole way in all our relating. **Every single gift given by God works together with every other gift given to form this cohesive and powerful thing we call redemption.** And it is at the point of redemption that your free will kicks in and you start your co-operation with God to unleash all the potential He placed in you uniquely.

The Holy Spirit is the most incredible aid to our empowered living and we'll explore throughout the book the inherent power and growth offered to us by Him. But He is so much more to us. He is the evidence of God with us – God's embrace in which He holds us. **Your whole life as a believer is folded in this 'embrace' which creates the miraculous 'environment' in which you live out your life.** Acts 17:28 "For in him we live, and move, and have our being ... For we are also his offspring."

Nourishing and growing.

It's aptly named Fruit of the Spirit because it bears fruit in your life that works inwardly and outwardly. **The Spirit flows through you, restoring you and others and expanding and increasing your inner and outer life.** It brings perfect balance to our emotional realm and centres us in the rest and refreshment promised by God to us through the Spirit. There is a rest involved in the Baptism in the Spirit because we are in communion with and led by the Holy Spirit. We don't have to strive or fret because we are kingdom heirs, with the Spirit in our lives and working on our behalf. We have the Gifts manifested and the Fruit evident in us. The more yielded in faith we are to the leading of the Spirit, the more all the blessings of the Spirit will manifest and the greater the empowerment released. This means that life becomes filled with the empowering of God for every deed and all events. It's smooth living. **Each gift given by God is effective according to God's plan for your life, uniquely.**

The great power and ability within the Gifts are tempered and honed through the Fruit of the Spirit. That is God's intention. The perfect balance and operation of the Gifts is locked into the balancing power of the Fruit working uniquely in your life. **By living in this balance of all that's available to us, we truly live in a place where "all things are possible to them that believe" because we can harness all the potential of our minds and all our physical abilities and co-operate with the Spirit's power.**

If you've never operated in the Gifts or feel you lack the Fruit of the Spirit in your life, now is the time to change that. Many believe that the Gifts were released only to start the Church, but it's evident throughout the scriptures that all but two of the Gifts were fully operational throughout the Old Testament. It's also clear throughout the bible that the Spirit has always been involved in the affairs of people, empowering and guiding them in life-changing ways.

Don't be robbed of the privilege of living an empowered life in the Holy Spirit, without measure, any longer! Pray and ask to be used in these Gifts and to manifest the Fruit of the Spirit in your life as a testimony to the indwelling Spirit and confirmation of the power of the work of Christ. Luke 11:13 "If you then, being evil, know how to give good gifts to your children, how much more will your heavenly Father give the Holy Spirit to those who ask Him?"

Here is a simple prayer to help you start:

"Matchless and boundless Father God, giver of great and wonderful gifts. Thank you for the gift of Jesus to restore my fellowship with You. Thank You for accepting me into Your kingdom and giving me a life with you. Thank You for all the blessings and benefits I have because you love me and walk with me. Thank You for the gift of your Holy Spirit as my Guide, my Helper and my Friend. Use me as a conduit of the Gifts and the Fruit of the Spirit as a testimony of the indwelling Spirit and confirmation of the power of the kingdom. Thank You for hearing and always answering my prayer. In Jesus' name. Amen."

Romans 8:14 & 17 "For as many as are led by the Spirit of God, these are children of God…and if children, then heirs – heirs of God and joint heirs with Christ."

So, what are we joint heirs with Jesus to?

INHERITED POWER

"For all the promises in Him (Jesus) are yes and in Him amen to the glory of God through us." 2 Corinthians 1:20

The earliest mention in the bible of Jesus sharing the redemptive message was in Matthew 4:17. Jesus starts His revelation of the gift God is giving in Him by declaring the kingdom is at hand. This is Him introducing Himself and His message. His focus is not on Himself but the kingdom for a very important reason.

While on earth, Jesus kept telling stories about the kingdom of heaven to communicate the great mystery of God with us and what that means. Matthew 13:34-35. He reveals to His followers that the presence of God was at hand in Him. This is important because in order for them to understand what Jesus is about to give them and how to operate in it, they would need to understand the fullness of the kingdom.

His disciples had knowledge revealed to them by Him about the power in this reality of the kingdom of heaven and understood that its dynamics released great abundance. **Jesus was bringing them to the living knowledge that the kingdom of heaven or kingdom of God** (used interchangeably in the bible) **is present whenever the King is present.** That means all the power, ability, glory, presence and every other imaginable part of the kingdom of heaven was at the disposal of Jesus through the Spirit. He tells them in Luke 17:21 "the kingdom of God is in your midst."

This is one powerful statement that Jesus is communicating. If the kingdom of heaven is where God is and the Spirit is right here where we are, that means all of God's presence and power is also in our midst. **Jesus was showing that the redeemed live and move and have their being inside the heavenly kingdom and have access to all of it through the Spirit.**

In Ephesians 1:3 Paul explains that "God has blessed us with every spiritual blessing in the heavenlies in Christ Jesus," by the indwelling spiritual presence of Jesus Christ after the new birth. The writer to the Hebrews indicates that believers have become "partakers of a heavenly calling" Hebrews 3:1, have "tasted of the heavenly gift" Hebrews 6:4, and have "come to the heavenly Jerusalem" Hebrews 12:22-24. **God has drawn the redeemed close so that we can hear and feel His love and He surrounded us with all of heaven's resources and revelation, 'living and being' in the kingdom.** Jesus will demonstrate the kingdom as a flesh and blood man so that we can know for sure that as believers we too, have the ability to live in this empowered state.

The message Jesus is bringing is so that you and I will have the full perception shift to go with our new birth and inhabit and live fully in touch with God and His goodness.

1 John 5:6 & 8 "This is He who came by water and blood - Jesus Christ; not only by water, but by water and blood. And it is the Spirit who bears witness because the Spirit is

truth … And there are three that bear witness on earth: the Spirit, the water, and the blood; and these three agree as one." The Spirit, water and blood agree and bear witness about the completed work of the birth, life, death and resurrection of Jesus Christ that revealed God, restored communion and released the kingdom in our midst.

Jesus sets about demonstrating how to know and live in this kingdom of heaven throughout His life. Every miracle and reference to God contain glimpses of this kingdom and the incredible abundance it contains.

The access point to the kingdom is to be where God is. When Peter had the revelation that Jesus is the Saviour, Son of the living God, Jesus tells Him the knowledge was revealed to Peter by God the Father in heaven. This is the revelation, God with us, that Jesus declares to be the foundation on which He will build His church. **And this revelation of God with us also means that the kingdom of God is with us with all its inherent power and possibility.**

Matthew 16:19 "And I will give you the keys of the kingdom of heaven: and whatsoever you bind on earth shall be bound in heaven: and whatsoever you loose on earth shall be loosed in heaven." Put another way, by having the keys to the kingdom you have free access to come and go as you please and you have the authority and power to alter the course of the world. What you set in motion will be honoured in heaven! This is what is available to you as a joint heir of God.

Wow! Look at that verse again. That's a lot of power given to anyone who understands who Christ is and what the kingdom means. And Jesus chose to reveal Himself and the power of the kingdom of heaven to humanity as a human so that we, as human beings, could identify and realise that we too, can live in the fullness of our inheritance.

His revelation of the mystery of the kingdom to the future heirs of the kingdom enables us to function and live from within the power and presence in the kingdom.

Every place you live has rules that guide the land that must be understood and followed and the kingdom of heaven is no different. In order to live in the kingdom we must understand the kingdom reality that where God is, all of the kingdom possibility is. So, God in us and with us ensures we are surrounded by and have access to all of the kingdom. Learning how to access all this is something we undertake and this requires a perception shift from us and an acknowledgement of who and what we fundamentally are...

Multi-Dimensional Living

Blending life in two worlds.

You live and move and have your being (Acts 17:28) in more than one realm because you are a multi-dimensional being. You are a spirit with a mind that lives in a body. You function and live your life in all three places at the same time. There are physical laws that apply to the physical realm, like gravity. There are mental laws that apply to your soul realm and there are spiritual laws that apply to the spirit realm. All these laws and realms are subject to the kingdom rules and each area only works in harmony with the others through it.

Being body-based in a world that is always on and pinging for your attention, how do you balance this so you can thrive? **It's easy to reduce bible study to the realm of the**

intellectual or spiritual and end up living out of touch and stagnant while God and the world continue dynamically. By embracing the reality that we are multi-dimensional and that we live multi-dimensional lives, we can truly inhabit all parts of our lives and enjoy living.

With the help of the Spirit and operating through our kingdom thinking, we use what John Stott called 'double listening'. Its listening both to the Spirit and to the world, in order to be able to relate one to the other. **This is important because you, as an eternal being, will be working out your destiny in the finite physical world. And that is going to require all three realms of spirit, mind and body working together in your life.**

The process of double listening won't necessarily be comfortable because the Word and the world are fundamentally in tension. We have to be 'in the world but not of the world', John 17. And although we are not of the world we are bound by its laws and we live bodily in the physical realm. There are both engagements with the world and a degree of separation from it. By combining our worldly knowledge with the wisdom of the bible, our double listening allows us to operate in the fullness of both. We take advantage of what both offer to expand our lives. In order to apply the bible to a particular area of life, we have to know that area well. **How can you expect to understand a biblical approach to, say, the economy and how to prosper, without a certain level of economic literacy?** If you don't have this knowledge how could it effect your ability to fund your destiny and that of others? Double listening will help you to listen to both and the Fruit and the Gifts will help you live in both in mental wholeness and power.

Aligning the dimensions.

Everything is interlinked for us as believers because we live multi-dimensionally. Let's get to grips with the concept. Take a sheet of paper and roll it up and hold it in your hand. Imagine inside this is the 'time tunnel', the place where we live out a linear life. Both time and space as we know it were created (Genesis 1:1 & 3) with the time tunnel, which is a created space. **But all around this time tunnel is eternity without the linear limitations of time and space. It functions unrestricted and unlimited.** Even though we are living in this time tunnel, we were meant to **enjoy and live physically, with total identification and recognition of the tangible and fully function and live in the eternal dimension.** Hebrews 11:3. These two diverse existences (physical and spiritual) are spanned by the bridge of the mind. By training your 'mind bridge' you bring these dimensions into alignment. **This 'mind bridge' is directing your actions and will determine how many of the gifts of the Creator, available to you in these dimensions, are used by you.** Your 'mind bridge' will either allow or deny you access to the gifts and blended living.

Living an effective multi-dimensional life does take effort from you. You're changing the programming of your thinking and your perspective in an environment filled with noise and distraction. It requires training the mind to understand and function in these dimensions. **This is intuitive living, with thought and feeling connected in the moment to create your life and live in an 'open awareness' state.** Living like this releases all the power of your amazing creative brain into your life. This is powerful, whole living. The Creator's gift for us to allow us to live our multi-dimensional lives as fully empowered and happy multi-dimensional beings.

2 Peter 1:3-4 "as His divine power has given us all things that pertain to life and godliness, through the knowledge of

Him who called us by glory and virtue, by which have been given to us exceedingly great and precious promises, that through these you may be partakers of the divine nature..." **You operate in the divine nature of God, and your life is the living story that shows the power of redemption and restoration that goes beyond eternal life to the place of the restored beauty of the image and likeness of God in us.** This is an eternal gift to you and only you can limit its manifesting in your life.

You have help and encouragement through other believers in your fellowship. We are commissioned by Christ Himself to work as a unified whole. To achieve this, Jesus gave gifts to the Church just before He ascended to heaven to ensure that the Body He loves functions effectively. These gifts all take on different aspects of Christ Himself to help the Body "grow up" into the perfection that's fit to be called the Body of Christ.

Ephesians 3:19-20 "to know the love of Christ which passes all knowledge; that you may be filled with all the fullness of God. Now to Him who is able to do exceedingly abundantly above all that we ask or think, according to the power that works in us."

Ever opened a gift and found you needed batteries to operate it and that those were not included? **All God's gifts have the 'batteries' included!** As multi-dimensional beings living multi-dimensional lives, we have built-in abilities to grow in spirit, mind and body. Let's look at your built-in ability to grow, change and expand your life…

And...Stretch!

You got it, now use it.

This is basically what God said to Adam in the Garden of Eden. Let's take a closer look at what it means to us in our lives now, by looking back at what happened there.

Genesis 2:19 "Out of the ground the Lord God formed every beast of the field and every bird of the air and brought them to Adam to see what he would call them. And whatever Adam called each living creature, that was its name."

Adam was so aligned with God's thinking and creative abilities he could discern the very nature of creatures and name them according to their natures.

He understood that the name and the nature of a creature must match and release the potential of each creature's nature. **This was Adam operating in the fullness of his image and likeness of God, creating and releasing potential in the same manner as his Maker.** He was in partnership with God in the fullest way in this act, using his full capabilities.

Genesis 1:28 shows what it meant to have dominion over the earth: Adam and Eve governing creation in the intimate knowledge and understanding of the whole creation and God's plan and purpose for each part of it. **God gave them free rein to rule and develop the earth and to grow in their own knowledge of their abilities in the process!** They had the ability to do this because God had given them the gift of unlimited mental potential. And the Garden of Eden was the perfect environment to release the full potential of the mind! **They were to keep developing their environment and themselves to their fullest potential.**

We all know what happened next. They chose to give their potential away and in this disobedient act, lost the ability to think and act like God. **The mind that was the bridge that connected the spirit and the body to God and unlimited Godlike potential became the very instrument of separation from God.** The light of God in the spirit grew dim and went out and the mind no longer had the potential to grasp the reality of God or His mind. From naming a creation in the untarnished dominion of whole-being living to flesh-based shame and fear, Adam and Eve could no longer connect to the presence of God. Their minds were tarnished and melded with a dead spirit that could no longer discern the intangible and invisible in physical and manifested creation. **They lost the potential to think like God and live as multi-dimensional beings.**

The rescue plan conceived in the inner courts of heaven comes into effect and God as man steps into the time tunnel to show us the way back to our full potential and help us remember who we are. The spirit is made new and is reconnected to God at the new birth, with the light of God going back on in the spirit of the redeemed. Through this redemption, the image and likeness of God in us is fully restored. Hebrews 4:12-13 God divided soul and spirit the moment Jesus as the Word takes up residence in your heart. Your spirit is made new, but your mind remains the same. But in order to function in your full potential, you need your mind to work as God intended - in dynamic creative ability.

By harmonising our mind with our God filled spirit, the body falls in line with transformed living. You have a two thirds majority that is unstoppable and will cause your body to line up with your mind and your spirit! So, the mind is the key to getting this to happen in your life. (If you want to know more about your mind, read 'Create your New Mind' https://www.amazon.co.uk/dp/B07Y5WC9GW [4])

God, in His dealings with us, is never static. His interactions are dynamic and present in the moment, and that's where His power is for that moment. So, it follows that if we want to experience God in real time, we have to flow in our thinking just as the Creator who made our minds does. This takes training of the mind. Just like Adam, we gain dominion over the outer and inner world in order to inherit it and grow. 1 John 5:4.

All of the kingdom of God is dynamic and active. So, we don't just stay in the same place when we're inactive or passive mentally, we lose ground.

The good news is that an active mind allows you to flow and function in the dynamic and active power of God. At any time in your life you can course correct or take off in a different direction. I had a client who described her life as the Titanic and so I reminded her that the Titanic sank as a result of human miscalculations and that at any time the Titanic could have been turned around and gone on to finish the journey in triumph. It changed her life. Change starts with a perception shift.

Creative Power.

Proverbs 4:23 "Keep your heart with all diligence, for out of it spring the issues of life."

Issues here literally means the source. We produce our treasure or life from the inside out, not the outside in. So, where exactly, inside of us, do we produce our treasure? Your heart is not the organ that acts as pump in your chest but the centre of you, your mind. It is the very core of you. Your heart (the centre of you, not the organ) is the central place from which everything in you flows outward, the control room of your life and being. The heart directs your actions and will determine how many of the gifts of the Creator are used by you. That heart power is working through you every day, with every thought you think, you are creating. Your heart is 'issuing' your life as Proverbs 4:23 states.

In order to create the optimum environment of growth, we use the mind to consciously create the 'issues', the flowing out, of our lives. Although many mind responses are internal or unconscious and relate to body functions and maintenance, others determine how we govern our inner and outer worlds.

The reason and purpose for this gift to you is to enable you to create from within, outwardly. While quietly sitting reading this, you're bringing into existence relationships and events in your life. Even when we're not aware of what we're creating and how we're influencing our environment we're still influencing it! Our minds treat our thoughts as real and tangible and bring bodily and mental responses to the reality of this place and moment in time. Like God, you think and then respond to that thinking by creating.

This is the power of your mind (the centre of you) functioning in your life on a daily basis. Your mind is creating because you have that ability placed in you by your Creator. Your mind gives you access to all the potential latent in you and much more. God purposely 'built in' these abilities in you so you would be able to use your mind to connect your physical living with your spiritual power!

The Potential Point.

The potential is there in each of us but we have to learn how to use it. The way to reconnect is through redemption because it brings life back to our spirit and opens our minds to the life-giving power and potential of God. Like opening your eyes and suddenly seeing all the colour, shapes and textures after just seeing the dark of your own eyelids! **But just like our ancestors in the Garden, we have to keep developing our environment and ourselves to our fullest potential. We grow in our ability to think and act like God.**

2/3 of the New Testament is made up of instructions relating to the mind in some form or the other. **The New Testament writers, under the inspiration of the Holy Spirit, wanted to take the believer beyond the knowledge and fact of redemption to a place of wholeness in living and life.** The way we treat ourselves internally often spills over into the way we treat others. It also hugely affects how effective we'll be in living fully in what we want. **This is the exciting area we're bringing change to so that all the potential of your internal voice is trained to default to growth, love, positive change and wellbeing.** You're thinking all the time, you're just training to think in the best way.

By taking charge of your inner world and surrendering it to the cleansing power of the Holy Spirit and the washing of the Word, you are changing your thinking patterns, and through your effort, creating the new mind in line with your renewed spirit. You take the mental realm captive! To ensure we can do that God gave us this incredible mind to co-operate with the Spirit to operate at the same level Adam did in his creative naming in the Garden. And our minds are made to continue to grow and expand throughout life. Your brain will help you do this.

'We each have 100 billion neurons in our brains – the brain's building blocks – and each neuron has between 1,000 to 10,000 connections to other neurons. These connections are known as neural pathways...The brain retains the ability to literally grow throughout a lifetime... The brain is, in fact, 'soft-wired', a term coined by renowned neuroscientist Dr Michael Merzenich. **This ability to adapt is called neuroplasticity.** The implications are quite profound – we might have much more ability to transform aspects of our personality than we realise. **We're not stuck with the brains we were born with and we're not trapped in patterns of thinking or behaviour, however ingrained they might seem.** In other words, you can teach an old brain new tricks.'[2]

Brain plasticity is one of God's ways to ensure that we have the mental capability to create and live at full kingdom potential.

Your mind develops from what you do as well as your behaviour. It's about putting what we learn into action in the knowledge that this will feed back into that development. Repetitive action goes hand-in-hand with and reinforces belief and understanding. Like a book that falls open at the same place because we've gone back to the same page over and over, the mindset becomes more and more habitual and normal. This causes us to live well-worn habits unthinkingly, in a state of mindless, repetitive action instead of wide-awake real-time living. But it can also work the other way. As we establish new habits that are life enlarging, these in time, will become well-worn and become our new default setting. **Living at peak potential becomes second nature and we can do it effortlessly.**

You can take charge and use brain plasticity to change and enhance the quality of your life.

The best driver of brain plasticity in your brain is your behaviour, and your brain is shaped structurally and functionally by events you do or don't do. Let's say you decide to learn to play an instrument and in your first session you really start getting it but then the next day you have forgotten most of it. Has this ever happened to you when you're learning something new? This happens because your initial short-term learning is spurred chemically in the brain, specifically for short term use. Structural change in your brain comes through practising the instrument. **Over time, your brain structurally changes to accommodate your learned, integrated knowledge.** It becomes cell memory. A good example of this would be London cabbies who have to memorise the London map to obtain a cabbie licence. They have greater areas of their brains dedicated to spatial information. **This is physical brain change to accommodate mental growth.** Using your brain to expand and grow, just as Adam should've done.

Your mind is the bridge between your physical life and your spiritual life. This is the 'Bridge of Possibility'[3].

Your whole brain in concert uses chemical, structural and functional change in brain plasticity, but in a unique way in each brain, based on your individual biomarkers. Your incredible brain is an instrument that allows you to live a life of conscious choice and awareness. It's the power placed purposefully in you by your Creator to ensure you can choose an abundant, powerful, meaningful, creative life.

Your 'mind bridge' will either allow or deny you access to the gifts. It's ours, but we must want it and do our part to enjoy it. Remember, long term change in the brain comes through continued, repetitive behaviour. This means you take responsibility and make the time to do what you need to grow.

Your 'Bridge of Possibility' links you as a multi-

dimensional being. Your mind connects your physical body and life with your spiritual self and life and ultimately determines the course of your life.

Let's get down to what that means to you…

FRUIT, NOTHING BUT FRUIT!

A fruitful life flows from the right perspective.

Your perspective determines your reality. Not reality itself but your reality – the way you will live out your life. And belief is the core propelling force to bring you to the place of living in your full kingdom destiny. This isn't your belief in God that I'm talking about. This is what you believe about yourself and what God will do for you. Merely having mental assent and knowledge about your kingdom blessings won't create a fruitful life. You must be able to look at all that was given and be able to say, "Yes, this is mine now." believing it's true and living it.

In John 8:31-36 Jesus reveals how we live in the truth that makes us free: "Therefore, if the Son makes you free, you shall be free indeed." Jesus compares mere knowledge of biblical law to experiential knowledge. This is taking knowledge of the kingdom and living it because that's the only way you can truly 'know' something. And it is in that 'knowing living' that your belief determines your perspective and your perspective determines what you'll expect and strive for and how much freedom in kingdom abundance you'll allow.

Andrew and Newberg in studying the power of belief, write "my subjects often believe that they perceive a higher or deeper layer of reality to which they feel connected... From my research... **I have come to believe that the more one focuses on a certain belief, the more real it may ultimately feel, and that this sense of realness is based on the stimulation of specific neural circuits in the brain.** Emotions and sensory stimulation also accentuate this sense of realness... **What the research has found so far is that your perceptions of reality and your beliefs are inextricably intertwined."**[6] What you perceive as your reality, the things you believe true about your life, abilities, relationships, God, money, everything in your life and about your life, forms the foundation of your beliefs.

I believe...

The decisions you're making right now and every day about your life are based on your beliefs about your reality, and the possibilities that exist in your reality are defined by your beliefs. **Your personal inner world, your beliefs that you hold about yourself, the world around you, other people and God all fall into the perception you hold and therefore determine your reality.**

Sometimes by just living we pick up script errors without realising it and incorporate these as hidden errors into our life-story as beliefs. You also have many beliefs that were established during childhood, with other beliefs left over from situations and circumstances that are no longer relevant, but continue to restrict and limit you from making the changes you want in your life now. Beliefs that were once useful to you to some degree, may now be the same beliefs that imprison you and keep you away from achieving all that you desire and want. These limiting beliefs get in the way of living in the unrestricted power the Spirit offers.

Jesus gave us a blueprint to freedom from limiting beliefs in John 8:31-36: knowing living - a life lived in the full understanding of the truth of kingdom power and possibilities daily. By truly knowing all the promises and truth of God is yours right now, you have an anchor point that will form the core to all of your life – you live from the right perspective. **This means that no matter what you're facing in your life, good or bad, abundance or lack, health or sickness, your reality remains that all the kingdom is working in your life every day and you intentionally tap in.** You expect it to be evident in your life every day. You live looking and acting like Jesus.

2 Peter 1:3-4 "as His divine power has given us all things that pertain to life and godliness, through the knowledge of Him who called us…given to us exceedingly great and precious promises, that through these you may be partakers of the divine nature…"

The biology of belief is working all the time and shows just how powerful belief is in determining our life outcomes – the fruit your life produces. Because your beliefs shape your life, your beliefs can actually heal you, both mentally and physically. Beliefs are powerfully affecting and driving your life. How? Through your thinking.

Your thoughts are the voice of your beliefs.

Psalm 139:23 "Search me, O God, and know my heart; Try me, and know my thoughts…" Why is it important to know your thoughts?

You have a continuous conversation going on with yourself. You're telling yourself your story. And because it's a familiar voice you hear, you trust it implicitly. Some of these statements you make to yourself form emotions, which in turn affect your actions, which affect the direction of your life. The powerful thing about this is that you can listen to what you're saying, take the time to uncover the beliefs behind the story and start inserting new scenes in your life-story.

By simply experiencing this moment, and living in this moment, as this moment, you allow your mind to respond creatively to something that is real instead of something from the past. The more you do this, the less you'll be influenced by stories of the past. I've had many clients and students who'd come to my sessions some months into counselling with huge grins and report that when they had a belief manifesting, they laughed and said to themselves: "That's not true". That simple realisation usually moved them into new directions and the success intensified their desire to keep changing their inner world to live a whole and happy life. **They changed only one thing - their perception of their reality which exposed the false belief which they could replace with a true one.**

The Israelites accepted a physical deliverance from the bondage of slavery in Egypt but remained slaves mentally. They had built that belief about themselves and were unwilling to let go of it, even in the face of a great, delivering God. That affected their choices in life and their relationship with God and those about them. And that in turn had consequences in their lives – wandering in the desert for 40 years. Beliefs can be either liberating or binding – we decide which through the power of our free will and choices we make.

Mental positioning.

Your 'mental position' is the way you exercise your mind and what you allow place in your mind, which influences the direction of your mind and consequently, your life. **It's all in the way you use what you have.** Although the Israelites had been freed from slavery by mighty, indisputable acts of God, their minds remained in the story of slavery. They thought of themselves as slaves and told themselves that story. Their perception of themselves and their accompanying belief is captured vividly when the 12 spies return to report back on the land God promised them in Numbers 13:32 - 33.

With the prospect of a land flowing with milk and honey and the recent history of the great miracles of deliverance, their perspective of themselves is as helpless and small. Their perception of themselves is grasshoppers and consequently, their reality is that they're little, not only in their own sight but in the sight of those they met. Contrast their response with Caleb and Joshua who saw the very same giants and the very same land. Numbers 13:30 "Then Caleb quieted the people before Moses, and said, 'Let us go up at once and take possession, for we are well able to overcome it.'" Ask yourself, why is their response so different?

Our perspective and perception we hold of ourselves determines our reality in all ways. **One profound way is the way we project and the imperceptible messages we send to others subliminally about who we think we are.** Those around us 'pick up' on the message we convey about ourselves and respond to us based on that and not on the reality of who we actually are supposed to be. The Israelites' perception of the Promised Land and Jehovah God was different from Joshua and Caleb, therefore, their reality looked completely different. **And those they encountered in the land treated them according to what they thought of themselves, not what God had said they were.**

So, even after we've seen the hand of God mightily in our own lives and know the power of both redemption and the great Redeemer, we can still choose to stay in a small story. Although the spirit inside of us was made new at adoption, the mind seeks to continue its old patterns of thinking, believing, imagining and remembering. And the will seeks to determine its own way and lead us according to our own thinking. **Because this is the way we have behaved all of our lives, it is, to us, a natural state, a life habit, if you will, that we must replace with the true natural state of mind we should have.** This takes action and decision on our part. The body will follow the mind unless you consciously decide and act contrary to the old ways and train your mind to align with your renewed spirit. **Changing your perception takes the courage of changing.** And in this change, everything will change in degrees.

Double-mindedness prevents us from receiving from God - we can't think like royalty and slave at the same time - the thought patterns and actions of these two are completely opposite. The power God gave us was choice. We choose which stories we live and tell ourselves and what we believe. What we choose to give our intellect to attain or fully know will determine the conclusions we have about life and how fully we live it. We've been given everything we need to bring about the changes to enter into whole and happy living.

Changing your reality.

Your mental 'place' in your own inner world, determines your perception, your awareness. And your perception determines your reality. This is the first great key to mind renewal. **By changing the perception you've held, you're able to change your reality.** Please note, your reality - not reality itself. By changing your reality, you change your intention and thinking about your life and build the beliefs that line up with the gifts God has given you.

Proverbs 23:7a "For as he thinks in his heart, so is he."

Our inner world will determine our outer world. Listen to your own inner dialogue and then ask yourself: What's the evidence for this thought? Is it really true? Is it the whole story? What more rational, balanced thought could I put in its place? Does this line up with what I know about the kingdom? How do I need to think about this so that it lines up with my new mind? How should I think and act in this situation to be like Jesus? Use these types of questions to challenge the limiting perspective and belief inside yourself. **By incorporating incremental changes in awareness and simple self-questioning techniques, you're creating your new mind that brings change that can be measured in your life and actions and in your brain.**

Looking at your beliefs you'll uncover some areas you believe that you're failing in. Redefine failure as an unacceptable outcome and reframe any skills you haven't yet mastered by telling yourself "this hasn't happened... **yet**". By incorporating this simple statement into your inner belief system you've liberated your incredible mind to go to work on finding a way for it to happen. So, when you encounter these areas, use this sentence: "this hasn't happened... yet", and keep going!

Here is my gift that you can use as a tool to help you clarify your thinking on how you want to live. https://thefluidway.com/wp-content/uploads/2020/08/Destiny-Living-Toolkit.pdf

You are building your future beliefs that will impact every area of your life. Apart from prayer and yielding to the Spirit of truth to light up the areas to change, you have to be willing to honestly look at yourself to change and follow through with action. **By learning to find and change pathological** (diseased) **beliefs, thoughts and attitudes, you can replace them with a truth-filled and a healing mindset.** That radiates out into all your life, your relationships, your success - a fruitful life lived from the right perspective.

With your perception change and healthy beliefs, you can live and access all the power of the Fruit and tap into all the power of your mind…

Fruitful Thinking

You produce your life from the inside out, not the outside in.

Your mind, the centre of you, is the reservoir you draw on throughout this journey we call life. It points you where to go, directs your actions and the course of your life. Your mind will determine the choices you make and the consequences you live with as a result of those choices. **As a result, your mind actively impacts your life.**

We produce our treasure or life from the inside out, not the outside in. Ultimately, it's not talent or fame or any outward thing that determines effective kingdom living, it's the treasure inside. As we all have potential, it's the 'mix' or 'bent' of the mind that takes the unlimited potential and grows fruit.

Jesus relates the fruit of a life to what's in the heart or the core of a person.

Matthew 12:35 "A good man out of the good treasure of his heart brings forth good things, and an evil man out of the evil treasure brings forth evil things."

Your mind is the most powerful tool you possess. It

connects the physical to the spiritual and determines how you live as a multi-dimensional being. The mind produces, it creates. **The treasure is good or defective, depending on whether the inner world is untarnished in Christ or diminished in wrong.** Living in the full belief of the kingdom as a multi-dimensional being empowered by the Spirit, we "put on the new man who is renewed in knowledge according to the image of Him who created him." Colossians 3:10. The new person is renewed in knowledge of the image of God. We know the possibilities that exist in having the image and likeness of God restored in us because we know what Adam was capable of. Renewed in knowledge allows you to think like God. How do we 'put on' the new?

1 Corinthians 2:16b "But we have the mind of Christ."

Having the mind of Christ doesn't mean that we're using the mind of Christ. Let me illustrate. I can have ten million dollars in the bank and be called a millionaire but if I never use that money to benefit myself, my family, the Body of Christ and the world, it's worthless. **We must yield the use of our minds to renewed knowledge of the image of God in us to live in the benefits of having the mind of Christ.** Colossians 3:10.

We will not think or live beyond the borders our inner world frames around our lives.

Philippians 2:5 "Let this mind be in you, which was also in Christ Jesus." Jesus lived a life of potential, transforming those He met and changing the world. The way Jesus used His mind is available to us to copy.

We cannot have God's fullness if we do not relinquish the entire mind to be overlaid and inhabited by the mind of Christ. An overlay is a transparent sheet that is placed over an existing structure to show the details that complete and furnish the structure. With the overlay of the mind of Christ we fully have the ability, with our minds to think, feel and act like Christ! We operate within our kingdom belief and access the power of the Fruit of the Spirit to live in wholeness exactly like Jesus did.

Don't look back, you're not going that way.

Romans 12:2 "And do not be conformed to this world, but be transformed by the renewing of your mind, that you might prove what is that good, and acceptable, and perfect will of God." This is fruitful thinking.

There is a renovation, a renewal that continues in your mind as you yield to the overlay of the mind of Christ. **It influences and changes the way you think, act and look now and in the future, it also changes the way you think, act and look back into the past.** Like it or not, the past influences now for us, and for those around us, and it dictates our future. So, when we overlay the mind of Christ onto our restored mind, we must yield the past to that overlay as well. Of course, we cannot change the past. **But we must change the way we view our past, including the actions, thoughts and how we looked back previously.** In order to live in a place of potential, we have to be able to see ourselves for who we really are and deal with the skewed image and beliefs of ourselves and others we've lived with.

Prayer and the Spirit will reveal what you need to address and guide you to the psychological tools to help you make the mental changes needed. You should also talk to someone you trust who can provide you with insight and another perspective. We all have blind spots, things we don't see about ourselves or that we treat as 'part of the furniture' in our thinking. Getting a fresh pair of eyes on this can be, well, eye opening.

The evidence of redemption is the fruit of a sound mind producing after its Maker.

2 Timothy 1:7 "For God has not given us a spirit of fear, but of power and of love and of a sound mind."

A 'safe mind' is what sound mind means in this verse. You have safe thinking that's revealed in good and wise judgment, disciplined and fruit producing thought patterns and the ability to understand right and to make right and fruitful decisions that enlarge your life and prosper you. The more you train your mind and think like Christ by fully connecting your mind to achieve the full release of the deposit God placed in your mind, the more you look and achieve like Christ. **You remember how to think like God.** We co-operate with God to make this happen by creating our new minds – putting off the old and putting on the new.

We seek to find God's ways to act, react and respond to life and everything in it. This is called mind renewal and requires a new mind. We wash our minds with the water of God's word to purify and transform it into operating in the overlay of the mind of Christ. **And we also use the psychological tools available to create new pathways in our thinking and our acting and change our doing.**

Colossians 3:9b-10 "…since you have put off the old man with his deeds and have put on the new man who is renewed in knowledge according to the image of Him who created him."

It's a three part process: we put off the old through action, allow the Holy Spirit and the Word to renew thinking and we put on the actions, beliefs and thoughts of a mind that thinks like God. **This scripture states that you put off. Putting off is a conscious action you decide to take.** Why is this important?

39

Living this way means finding new ways to think about your beliefs, time and actions.

2 Corinthians 10:3-5 "For though we walk in the flesh, we do not war according to the flesh. For the weapons of our warfare are not carnal but mighty in God for pulling down strongholds, casting down arguments and every high thing that exalts itself against the knowledge of God, bringing every thought into captivity to the obedience of Christ."

We mould our thinking to God's. **We put off and put on. In other words, we remember what we truly look like and were created to be on the inside.** We move from a life lived marred and limited by the effect of wrong thinking and wrongdoing and the broken nature, to thinking and acting like God.

Yet, we don't only want to change our old mind away from things of our past, we also want to release the power placed in us to improve our future. We want to unleash all the power and potential in our 'Bridge of Possibility'. It's training the mind in the thinking that leads to power and transformation that gives us the foundation to operate in power and wholeness. And this is our part in doing.

Think 'right'.

The mind's creation is thoughts and thoughts determine the inward and outward realities, the 'how we think and how we then respond to what we think' in our lives. So, your thoughts are coloured by your programming and in how you think and how you then respond to what you think. Any areas you are experiencing that hold you back can, with careful thought, some prayer, the Spirit and psychological tools become a place of growth and triumph. It starts with you getting to know yourself and how you think.

Quality, daily quiet time is so important so you can connect to self and to God. It gives you time to stop and listen and look at your thinking and the result of your thinking and actions in your life. Honesty, willingness to change and listening both to what you find and what God tells you are the keys to the growth you'll have. On top of that, you'll be pleasing to God who loves an open heart that's ready to listen, grow and change. I don't know about you, but I tend to give my gifts, wisdom and knowledge to those who listen, appreciate and respond. So, if you're ready and open, don't you think you'll find that God rewards this handsomely?

'Put Yourself in Order'.

The potential of expanding your life and living in the full power and potential of your mind is already yours in this moment. You can think like Jesus.

2 Corinthians 13:11 "Finally, brethren, farewell. Become complete. Be of good comfort, be of one mind, live in peace; and the God of love and peace will be with you." This is the word for how we exercise our minds, what thoughts or realities we entertain and follow. Paul's final exhortation in this letter more closely reads: 'Put yourself in order'. **It is a very definite command that requires very definite action from us.** And it happens right now.

What do you do with what you possess? The reality of all you know at this juncture must now be mixed with action *in this moment.* **Self-awareness puts your mind in the present - what you're doing in your responses and interactions and relating in this moment.** You are face to face with yourself and you're learning new things about yourself. It's a powerful place to live that has many benefits cascading off from it. For example, one amazing benefit is that self-awareness helps and improves your physical brain.

Brain change by being here, now.

A Harvard study states that being present and aware by living in this moment and using simple breathing exercises: "… is all it took to stimulate a major increase in grey matter density in the hippocampus, the part of the brain associated with self-awareness, compassion, and introspection." The study also found: "Participant-reported reductions in stress also were correlated with decreased grey-matter density in the amygdala, which is known to play an important role in anxiety and stress." God made you to live in this moment and so create your life and experience living in real time.

Your thoughts and how you think are coloured by, and interconnected to, your inner world. **The bible defines heart as 'the centre of anything'. It's the mind network within yourself that you use to respond to the world and everything in it.** As a matter of fact, it's because of your mental wiring in your mind network that you think thoughts the way you do.

Do you believe you can grow into something new?

It comes down to what mindset you choose to adopt. Stanford professor of psychology, Carol Deck, speaking of a growth mindset says it's characterised by a belief that your most basic abilities are not fixed or innate but can be developed. A fixed mindset, on the other hand, presupposes that talent is innate and that you are either good at something or not, leaving little room for humility, curiosity, learning or growth. **From Adam to you, God made all of us with the ability to grow, develop, expand, create and relate.**

Romans 12: 2 "And do not be conformed to this world, but be transformed by the renewing of your mind, that you may prove what is that good and acceptable and perfect will of God." The more we do this the more the old ways diminish, and the new mind is established. **The real you will take over.** The Holy Spirit will be with you every step of the way to empower, restore and guide you.

The Fruit filled life oils the tracks of our lives and allows the flow of the Gifts.

Remember, the Fruit works Spirit to mind. To fully enable it in our lives, we must do what is needed mentally, to release the power of the Spirit to flow through us. Each and every manifestation of the Fruit of the Holy Spirit requires a yielded and submitted life. Yielding to the manifestation of the Fruit of the Spirit means we surrender to the working power of the Fruit and seek to create opportunities to oil the tracks of our lives to the flowing and continuous manifestation of the Fruit and the Gifts. We do the mental work to change dysfunctions and wrong thinking to bring about the change and liberate our full potential.

Because we live in a tactile world, the tangibility of the kingdom of God can feel distant. The Holy Spirit is your contact point and compass as you navigate through life, and move in the possibility of your multi-dimensional kingdom living. The Spirit gives you the eyes to see the realm in all its glory and the guidance to access and grow in your inheritance. He also makes sure we don't lose sight of the kingdom or remain unaware of God's constant communion with us.

Jude 20 "But you, beloved, building yourselves up on your most holy faith, praying in the Holy Spirit." Accept what you have been given and think, act and speak in the power of the Spirit in the full knowledge of who you are!

Let's take a look at this great and wonderful gift: the Spirit at work in us…

THE CONTACT POINT

The Fruit only grows where the sap flows.

Jesus is the practical model for every believer. As God the Son, Jesus was something we can never be, but He lived His life as a human being. **The works Jesus did on earth He performed as a Spirit-endowed human.** Look at the ways that the Spirit met Jesus' needs and equipped Him to meet the needs of others. If Jesus Himself needed the Spirit's power, we do too, and it's available to us because God Himself took on flesh to come face to face with us and call us back to Him. **And He left us that face-to-face access through the indwelling Spirit. This same Spirit now flows from us to transform us and reveal the full power and glory of God and His kingdom to us.**

Romans 8:14 and 16 "For as many as are led by the Spirit of God, these are sons of God. The Spirit himself bears witness with our spirit that we are children of God." As an heir to a kingdom, you would live in a manner befitting the child of a king. You would receive instruction on how to govern what you will inherit and how to live and conduct yourself to bring honour to your king. In the kingdom of God, the Holy Spirit assumes the role of witness, testifying to the fact that you are, right now, a child of a king. This 'bearing witness' is both subtle and unseen, the inward working in you to train you into a close walk and relationship with God, and outward, like the manifestation of the Gifts and Fruit showing in your life.

A quick review of the Spirit shows a very intimate involvement with all creation and especially the heirs of the kingdom. In Genesis 2:7 God imparted some of His immortal Spirit into us and gave us the "quickening" of God. Job 33:4 "The Spirit of God has made me, and the breath of the Almighty has given me life." Humans were the creation between the angels above and the sensitive animals below. The physical body was formed as the living creatures from matter imbued with God's voice at creation; but his spirit was an immediate production of divine power. **In every part of our beings, we have the voice of God "upholding all things by the word of His power".** We are the crowning glory in this creation that receives God's image, **and because of what we are, we only function to the full image and likeness of God in us when we do so from within the kingdom.**

The Spirit is hovering over the earth just as He did at creation and we are living within that same creative power of the Spirit that was at work at creation. 2 Corinthians 3:18 "But we all, with unveiled face, beholding as in a mirror the glory of the Lord, are being transformed into the same image from glory to glory, just as by the Spirit of the Lord." This transformation to greater glory is happening every moment of your life as you understand your inheritance and assume more of the Christ-like nature as a kingdom heir. And the Spirit is with you throughout this process.

Jesus came to restore what was lost and show, by living example, the love and power inherent in kingdom living. He made God visible to us and the Holy Spirit takes centre stage to make Christ's redemptive and beautifying work visible to the entire world. **He will do this through demonstrations of His power of the Gifts and healing presence found in the Fruit.** We as the believers flow with the Spirit to establish and enlarge the kingdom of heaven and act as conduits for God's goodness, power and Presence.

Romans 8:2 & 10-11"For the law of the Spirit of life in Christ Jesus has made me free from the law of wrongdoing and death. ... And if Christ is in you... the Spirit is life because of righteousness. But if the Spirit of Him who raised Jesus from the dead dwells in you, He who raised Christ from the dead will also give life to your mortal bodies through the Spirit who dwells in you." **This Spirit empowerment works to help us think and live differently.**

The very Spirit of life that breathed life into the first human is working in you and through you to liberate, empower and enlighten you through direct access to God. **At the moment of redemption an infinite surge of life entered your spirit and effectively filled the place the spirit of death occupied. The law of wrong and death was overwhelmed by the Spirit of life - He continues to do that.** This life-giving Spirit gives a new way of life for a new creation (2 Corinthians 5:17) made possible by the Spirit of Life. **We can now live in the resurrection power of Christ where the operation of the Gifts of the Spirit causes our lives to become supernatural. And we can function in this supernatural life from a new mind and whole and balanced life through the Fruit.**

God ensured that a Spirit-led life would be perfectly balanced in the power of the Gifts and the wholeness of the Fruit. This is the work of the Holy Spirit. To explore the Holy Spirit's working fully and for an in-depth look at the

Spirit I suggest 'The Holy Spirit Book'.[1] Here we are focusing on the Fruit of the Spirit and how the Holy Spirit uses the Fruit to aid us in living in both the kingdom and the world simultaneously as multi-dimensional beings. **By accepting that what we do affects more than just this world, we can live in the world and affect it beyond this time and place.** This is a mindset, a way of thinking, that will help you decide and determine how you live. It's the paradigm shift of Romans 12, the renewing of the mind. Empowered by the Spirit, we use psychological tools, effective worldly knowledge and wisdom to use our time and our life to bring about our large kingdom life.

With the perception shift that comes through understanding our multi-dimensional life, we can live fully aware and function within the possibilities of kingdom living. We want to combine an understanding of the power available through the Spirit and how to access it through our perception shift so we can maximize our new mind's potential power…

Without Measure

Jesus left behind a clear message to us that what He established on earth is now ours to enjoy in our kingdom life here on earth and in the life to come.

Jesus is about to physically leave earth. Because the king was present on the earth, the kingdom of heaven was established on the earth in full power and remains here. This power will flow from being in Jesus to being available to all. Jesus set about to prepare His disciples for receiving the Spirit without measure – the Spirit unlimited. He trained them in the knowledge of the kingdom and they have seen the power of the kingdom through His ministry and their own ministry under His anointing. They are about to 'take on' the Spirit without measure and operate just as Jesus had shown them in kingdom living.

Just before His physical departure from earth, Jesus prepared His disciples to assume all the power and ability they had seen Him operating in John 20:21-22 "Then Jesus said to them again 'Peace to you! As the Father has sent Me, I also send you!' And when He had said this, He breathed on them, and said to them 'Receive the Holy Spirit.'" Notice Jesus combines an action with a command: They are sent out, so He empowers them.

Just as the Spirit moved before God created, He now moves to empower life and destiny. These disciples already had a saving knowledge of Christ although they didn't fully understand. They had operated in signs and wonders under Jesus' anointing, but now He prepares them to receive the Spirit fully. Before His departure, He instructs them to wait for the Spirit without measure that He had operated in. On the day of Pentecost, the Spirit without measure is poured out.

History repeats.

In the Garden of Eden, God had knelt beside a clay form and breathed the breath of life into it to make it His crowning glory. By His Spirit, He infused a form with His spiritual genetics and implanted His image in His creation Job 33:4. God has again knelt in earthly soil in the Garden of Gethsemane, and afterwards again He breathes the breath of His very Spirit into those who believe. This time, he does so to restore His image and likeness to the 'very good' that it was at creation and to release the Spirit to aid us in how we should live as joint-heirs in the kingdom.

The breath of change.

Jesus breathing on His disciples was the breath of change that would transform the world! He was preparing them for a level of power that they had only known through His anointing. They are about to be baptised in the Holy Spirit's unlimited power, so Jesus tells them 'tarry' (wait in expectation) until they receive the fullness Acts 1:5 & 8.

Luke 24:49 "Behold, I send the Promise of My Father upon you; but tarry in the city of Jerusalem until you are endued with power from on high." 'Endued' means to 'sink into a garment or to invest with clothing.' A surrender into and a putting on of the vestment and the office it represents. **Being endued with the Holy Spirit shows how He covers our human weakness and empowers and transforms us through the official vestment He gives, identifying us as divine representatives.** It's clearly evident in the spirit realm as it's the outward evidence of the inward work of the Spirit.

In seeking and operating in the fullness of the Spirit without measure, we have at our disposal all the wisdom and power of God Himself.

With the disciples, as with us, the purpose of this "enduing" is for us to assume the full flavour of Christ and become so imbued with Him that we can assume what He completed and live in the kingdom with the resident power of the Holy Spirit. We regain the ability Adam had when he named creation. **With this ability we will demonstrate through our lives all the power and possibility of the kingdom of God.**

The Holy Spirit received at salvation to prepare the way for the living Word in us, now goes to the next level with Baptism in the Holy Spirit to release the Spirit without measure. What does this look like? In the early formation of the Church each filling was accompanied by a sign. Acts 2:4 "And they were all filled with the Holy Ghost, and began to speak with other tongues, as the Spirit gave them utterance." The filling was accompanied by the sign of speaking in unknown language (a language they had not learnt). Acts 10:45-47 "while Peter spoke these words, the Holy Spirit fell on all of them who heard the word... For they heard them speak with tongues and magnify God..." This is the magnificent restoration God had promised. This sign was and continues to be part of the Baptism of the Spirit and was foretold in the Old Testament. God had spoken of this sign through His prophet.

Prophecy fulfilled.

Isaiah 28:10-12 "For precept must be upon precept, precept upon precept, Line upon line, line upon line, Here a little, there a little. For with stammering lips and another tongue He will speak to this people, to whom He said, 'This is the rest with which You may cause the weary to rest,' And, 'This is the refreshing'"

This level of the Spirit was foretold. In this picture given by the prophet Isaiah we see the overall purpose of the coming Baptism in the Holy Spirit. In order to assume what Christ completed and to build precept upon precept, expanding the knowledge and use of Christ's victory, we must speak and understand the other tongue God uses to speak to us. This promises a refreshing that comes through the building up in praying in our heavenly tongue and the systematic building of the kingdom.

Although speaking in our heavenly tongue is not a qualification for the Spirit without measure, it is an indication of the fullness and the empowerment of our mouths to become a creative unifying force. What, exactly does that mean and do we have biblical proof of this?

Restoring unity in creation.

Why does God have to release tongues and interpretation of tongues for the newly formed Body of Christ? **It's the mark of restoration from the division that happened at Babel. God re-unifies His creation not in one language but in one Spirit.** Let's look at what happened. Genesis 11:1 & 4 "Now the whole earth had one language and one speech," when man decides they want to break away from God.

God created humanity with a unified language because mankind was supposed to live with unified purpose in planetary guardianship, ruling in harmony and filling earth. However, humanity in their marred state chooses to use the power of one speech to establish themselves as a unified and identifiable force against God. **Mankind seeks to make a name apart from the Creator and establish a stronghold in one place only, instead of populating the whole world as God had commanded.**

Genesis 11: 6 & 9 "And the Lord said, 'Indeed the people are one and they all have one language, and this is what they begin to do; now nothing that they imagined to do will be withheld from them'… Therefore, its name is called Babel, because there the Lord confused the language of all the earth; and from there the Lord scattered them abroad over the face of all the earth." Note that God declares that 'nothing they imagine to do will be withheld.'

The power of speech.

As humans are created in the image and likeness of God,

we just like God, use speech to create, unify and relate. Different languages had to be in effect until the fullness of time when Jesus came to restore the image and likeness of God and birth the Body of Christ. In effect returning mankind to the place intended before the tower of Babel, where the unifying force of "nothing that they imagine to do will be withheld from them." **With the kingdom of heaven now on earth and the gift of this given, we can operate in the manner God intended when giving us one language.** Isaiah 28:10-12 is fulfilled with all the promise it entails.

So, we did not have one language system restored to us. Just as our fingerprints differ and our DNA is unique to each person, each person has a different and unique tongue. We were returned to the power of unified place because we operate through one Spirit. **In other words, it's our tongue and our vocal cords working with our faith, but it's the Holy Spirit who gives us substance or utterance.** This ensures that what we speak is the full and complete will of God. Now all the power of our unified ability in creating by speech is channelled through the perfect will of God for His purposes! It removes our agenda and our nature out of the equation of creating through the use of the tongue.

The Spirit and Prayer.

This is powerful living that Paul encourages. 1 Corinthians 14:14-15 "For if I pray in a tongue, my spirit prays, but my understanding is unfruitful. What is the conclusion then? I will pray with the spirit, and I will also pray with the understanding. I will sing with the spirit, and I will also sing with the understanding." So, you praying in your heavenly tongue is prayer from your spirit directly and uninterrupted through the Spirit.

Praying in the Spirit is not the only empowerment in

prayer that the Holy Spirit enables, but also when praying about a specific situation He can release specific details. The Holy Spirit can counsel you on how to pray for a certain situation so that you are in line with God's Word and desire. And the Spirit will help you discern if the answer is of God or not. Speaking in your heavenly tongue is tapping into the full access the Baptism of the Holy Spirit offers. It also connects you to the Gifts and the Fruit and how to flow and operate in both.

As tongues and the interpretation of tongues are the only two gifts of the Holy Spirit not manifested in the Old Testament, we know these are important to receive and operate in today as the Body of Christ living in kingdom life.

The disciples certainly recognised that tongues and interpretation of tongues was a sign of the Spirit without measure. They also recognised that this manifestation of the Spirit signified that these people were to be accepted as part of the Body of Christ as the Holy Spirit had sealed them through this sign.

Acts 10:44-47 "While Peter was still speaking these words, the Holy Spirit fell upon all those who heard the word. And those of the circumcision who believed were astonished, as many as came with Peter, because the gift of the Holy Spirit had been poured out on the Gentiles also. For they heard them speak with tongues and magnify God. Then Peter answered, 'Can anyone forbid water, that these should not be baptized who have received the Holy Spirit just as we have?'"

It's evident that the disciples considered the speaking in an unknown tongue as a sign of the Spirit without measure that came in the form of a baptism on those who believed. This was clearly a gift that went beyond the infilling of the Holy

Spirit that took place at salvation. As we have seen, the Gift of Tongues can be given directly by the hand of God, or through the medium of the laying on of hands.

It is important to note that the Spirit without measure gives us a continuous renewal and refilling to overflowing whenever we make ourselves available to Him. One of the greatest ways of drawing this overflowing into our lives is through prayer. It's quite extraordinary just how profoundly the Spirit uses praying in tongues. But every prayer, in our known language or in our heavenly tongue is empowered by the Holy Spirit. (To learn more about prayer and how to use the different types of prayer, read my book, 'Prayer Power')

The Spirit's work.

The Old Testament abounds with the gifts of the Holy Spirit working through all kinds of people as He wills. It's exciting to trace the manifestations of power and prophecy as they unfold, direct and guide the affairs of people. Seven of the gifts of the Holy Spirit operated in the Old Testament as powerfully as today. We see prophets such as Isaiah, Jeremiah and Daniel warning, exhorting and teaching God's chosen people. Elijah and Elisha are both used to raise the dead and manifest the gifts of healings and work miracles. Jacob operates in the discernment of spirits as he watches angels moving up and down the ladder to heaven and Gideon speaks to the Angel of the Lord face to face. Hebrews 11 gives us a gallery of those who operated in the gift of faith. Samuel uses the word of wisdom and the word of knowledge when he meets with Saul, assuring the lad that his father's donkeys are safe and preparing him for what is to come. The manifestations of the Gifts of the Spirit were operating throughout the Old Testament, powerfully declaring a very present God.

Only tongues and interpretation was given to the newly formed Body of Christ as a sign that the division caused at Babel because of the people's disobedience was removed. Although we have many different heavenly tongues we are now speaking by the same Spirit, not in one language but with one supernatural intent - the perfect will of God.

In the very evident presence of the sweet Spirit manifesting in unknown heavenly tongues, we also have the proof of the resurrection and glorification of Jesus.

Think on it. Tongues are the manifestation that we have received the Spirit without measure which we could not receive until Jesus completed the work and departed. John 7:39 "But this He spoke concerning the Spirit, whom those believing in Him would receive; for the Holy Spirit was not yet given, because Jesus was not yet glorified."

The early church considered speaking in tongues as a sign of the Spirit without measure and recognised that this meant the fullness of all the Spirit offers was given - The Gifts and the Fruit of the Spirit are released with all the power and wholeness.

In your life, right here and now, what does that mean? Let's take a look…

What do I do with this?

Living in the empowerment of the Gifts.

Ultimately all the ground we've covered in this book and all the empowerment we've uncovered must be effective in your life now. So, here is where you are as a kingdom believer right now:

•The kingdom is established and the possibility released to you as a multi-dimensional being living a multi-dimensional life.

•To live in this kingdom power you have to change your perspective about God, life and yourself so the reality you live is empowered by the Spirit.

• You have a brain that can do this.

•Kingdom living requires you to use and grow your mind – the bridge of possibility that links your physical and spiritual self to bring whole living in all three.

•You can operate your bridge of possibility in the mind of Christ.

•In order to assist you to achieve this, God gave you the Spirit without measure at the birth of the church and through this re-unified creation.

•The empowering of the Spirit assists our living through the power of the Gifts balanced by the healing wholeness of the Fruit.

What now?

Here we are. You have the Spirit without measure, you're speaking in tongues and you are empowered. You're good to go. So, what now? Well, the first step is to understand what the Gifts are and which of these are working in you uniquely.

1 Corinthians 12:8-11 "For to one is given by the Spirit the word of wisdom; to another the word of knowledge by the same Spirit, to another faith by the same Spirit; to another the gifts of healings by the same Spirit; to another working of miracles; to another prophecy; to another discerning of spirits; to another divers kinds of tongues; to another the

interpretation of tongues. All these work through the Spirit who gives to everyone as He wills."

With the earthly departure of Jesus ushering in the release of the Spirit without measure on the believers, the nine Gifts of the Spirit listed promote the kingdom and now have the specific task of profiting us as kingdom dwellers. 1 Corinthians 12:4-6 "Now there are diversities of gifts, but the same Spirit…it is the same God which works all in all. But the manifestation of the Spirit is given to every man to profit all." The word used for 'profit' can be interpreted as 'a bringing together' and 'benefit to' the Body of Christ, leading to direction and power for the empowering of every believer in kingdom living. These Gifts work beyond empowering the individual and into the larger community of kingdom believers.

A constant flow of power.

The nine gifts are given by the Spirit as He wills and will ebb and flow through all believers. So, if you are available to the Holy Spirit, the Gifts will flow through you. As the Gifts are given as the Spirit wills, some of the Gifts you operate in will only be for a time, but you also have definite Gifts for life. We can desire the other gifts and expect that the Holy Spirit will use us if we are willing and ready.

Some Gifts are imparted within a specific calling, gifting, or office to empower and propel the purposes of God within that ministering. Some empowerment may be for a period of time or for an assignment, but within the ascension gifts of apostle, prophet, evangelist, teacher and pastor, the gifts are permanent and have the Gifts of the Spirit specific to that office working all the time. For example, the office of prophet will operate in prophecy and many also manifest as word of wisdom and as word of knowledge. It's not limited to this because the Spirit decides as He wills which Gifts to impart as permanent deposit and which to give for a time or for an assignment.

Use the three.

The only three gifts that are constant and there for you, if you ask, are tongues, the interpretation of tongues, and prophecy with different depths of revelation. 1 Corinthians 14:1, 12 "Pursue love, and desire the spiritual gifts, but especially that you may prophesy. ... Even so you, since you are zealous for spiritual gifts, let it be for the edification of the church that you seek to excel." Paul is emphasizing that we should seek the Gifts to benefit the kingdom. He is bringing us back to the purpose of the Gifts: to empower the heirs of the kingdom and reveal the power and presence of God and eternal heaven.

1 Corinthians 12 shows the gifts operate for the profit of the whole Body. 1 Corinthians 12:1 describes gifts as 'things belonging to the Spirit'. It is by and through the Holy Spirit that we operate in these Gifts. We are told to desire these gifts because they are empowering for life and destiny. Knowing what is at your disposal uniquely in the Gifts will clarify your own spiritual 'wiring' and help you understand your personal destiny, your reason for being and how you fit in the kingdom.

How do you, specifically, fit into the Gifts and what are your unique blend of Gifts? Let's see...

A QUICK LOOK AT THE GIFTS

The Gifts work Spirit to spirit to empower your life and the life of the fellowship of believers with kingdom ability.

Part of the empowerment of the Spirit without measure is the Gifts. To understand what God has given you, we need to see the scope of these Gifts and how they manifest.

The nine Gifts of the Holy Spirit in 1 Corinthians 12:7-11 fall into three natural divisions.

Revelation gifts. They reveal or open certain aspects of a realm of the future, a realm of the present or past, or the realm of the spirit world. As with all Gifts of the Spirit, these are given as the Spirit wills, but the Spirit will always complement the five-fold ministry (ascension gifts) given by Jesus. So, if there's a strong five-fold ministry fulfilling their mandate set out in conjunction with the gifts given (Ephesians 4:11-16), the Gifts of the Spirit will be evident.

The three revelation Gifts

▪**Word of Wisdom.**

-The most prevalent manifestation in the church is a

revelation about a person or event to come which is usually preceded by a word of knowledge to raise faith and followed by prophecy or exhortation. This usually takes place in counselling or service and is directive – it's leading somewhere or taking the individual or group to a new perspective or dimension. The Holy Spirit reveals something past or present, raises faith, then releases a wisdom word that will affect the future, and finishes with the creative power of sealing it in prophecy. John 4:14-26 shows the woman at the well with Jesus and shows all these elements. He shows that He knows the man she is living with is not her husband and doesn't condemn but addresses her need and He sets the perfect example for how we should work in this Gift.

-Giving God's wisdom for an individual to deal with a situation or event. It's not reading the current events or situations but going to the core of the situation or event that isn't evident on the surface and knowing exactly what to do with the situation or event to turn it into a liberated or profitable or effective situation. The Spirit demonstrated this Gift in the life of Jesus before Jesus was born. Matthew 2:19-20 "But when Herod was dead, behold, an angel of the Lord appeared in a dream to Joseph in Egypt, saying, 'Arise, take the young Child and His mother, and go to the land of Israel, for those who sought the young Child's life are dead.'" Word of knowledge and wisdom work together, assuring Joseph that he can leave and telling him where to go.

-It may take a deep revelation that transforms the church or person and changes the course of events in their lives. God reveals His wisdom for a kingdom, global or prophetic event involving a group of people, a nation or globally. It may be an event, a judgment or a deep 'rhema' that transforms and alters the destiny or course of a people. John 2:19, 21 & 22 "Jesus answered and said to them, 'Destroy this temple, and in three days I will raise it up. ... But He was speaking of the temple of His body. Therefore, when He had risen from the dead, His disciples remembered that He had said this to them; and they believed the Scripture and the word which Jesus had said."

-God uses word of wisdom to release the calling to an individual or group and is usually accompanied with prophecy of what will be accomplished if the individual or group is obedient to the conditions. Acts 26:15-18 "So I said, 'Who are You, Lord?' And He said, 'I am Jesus, whom you are persecuting. But rise and stand on your feet; for I have appeared to you for this purpose, to make you a minister and a witness both of the things which you have seen and of the things which I will yet reveal to you. I will deliver you from the Jewish people, as well as from the Gentiles, to whom I now send you, to open their eyes and to turn them from darkness to light, and from the power of Satan to God, that they may receive forgiveness of sins and an inheritance among those who are sanctified by faith in Me.'"

-Rarely the gift is used to bring judgment or closure to a situation that could pose a danger or threat. 1 Corinthians 5:3 "For I verily, as absent in body, but present in spirit…" Or in the next scripture where this is used to bring closure to an earlier warning not heeded to raise their faith. Acts 27:23-25 "For there stood by me this night an angel of the God to whom I belong and whom I serve, saying, 'Do not be afraid, Paul; you must be brought before Caesar; and indeed God has granted you all those who sail with you.' Therefore, take heart, men, for I believe God that it will be just as it was told me."

▪Word of Knowledge.

-It has either already happened or is currently unfolding. This Scripture shows word of knowledge flowing naturally into word of wisdom. Luke 22:10-13 "And He said to them,

'Behold, when you have entered the city, a man will meet you carrying a pitcher of water; follow him into the house which he enters. Then you shall say to the master of the house, 'The Teacher says to you, 'Where is the guest room in which I may eat the Passover with My disciples?' Then he will show you a large, furnished upper room; there make ready.' So, they went and found it as He had said to them, and they prepared the Passover."

-Word of knowledge is not used as a teaching or preaching tool, nor can it be used to interpret the bible. No amount of ability or learning brings this word of knowledge. In a church or individual setting, it's taking the person or group beyond their knowledge and comfort zone to a new level in God. Matthew 16:16-17 "And Simon Peter answered and said, 'You are the Christ, the Son of the living God'...Jesus answered and said to him, 'Blessed are you, Simon Bar-Jonah, for flesh and blood has not revealed this to you, but My Father who is in heaven.'"

-The word of knowledge is used to direct someone to a blessing that the Spirit wants to bestow. This gift may also manifest by some knowledge of sickness or past event unknown to the speaker to raise the faith of the hearer to then receive healing or a word of wisdom or prophecy. Acts 9:11-12 "So the Lord said to him, 'Arise and go to the street called Straight, and inquire at the house of Judas for one called Saul of Tarsus, for behold, he is praying. And in a vision he has seen a man named Ananias coming in and putting his hand on him, so that he might receive his sight."

-As mentioned under wisdom, when the gift of wisdom is used in judgment or closure, the word of knowledge and at times even prophecy, works with it. When used in this circumstance it reveals the heart and character of the person or situation under judgment. Acts 5:1-10. All these elements are present in the revelation and judgment of Ananias and Sapphira.

-This Gift reveals deep truths about God, in revelation of the Father, Son or Holy Spirit, His Kingdom, or truths beyond what we can know. The Spirit often uses this Gift in the church to expand the vision of the church or the person or move the church or leadership out of their comfort zone. Ephesians 3:3-5 "how that by revelation He made known to me the mystery (as I wrote before in few words, by which, when you read, you may understand my knowledge in the mystery of Christ) which in other ages was not made known to the sons of men, as it has now been revealed by the Spirit to His holy apostles and prophets."

▪**Discerning of Spirits.** This gift deals strictly with the spirit realm. In the case of dealing with demonic situations, this Gift only discerns and it needs other Gifts for the casting out and deliverance. When revealing the angelic realm, it usually leads to revelation that is coupled with prophecy or praise.

-This Gift operates in all things that pertain to the spirit realm and will reveal the heavenlies of God and the realm of the fallen angels. Not all things revealed to us can be shared because of the limitation of human language. 2 Corinthians 12:4 "… how he was caught up into Paradise and heard inexpressible words, which it is not lawful for man to utter." Another reason why we needed tongues! Praying about what was revealed will often 'spread out' the revelation, with the Spirit giving us the information of what we are to do with the revelation. It's extremely important to have input from mature Christians versed in the Holy Spirit and the spirit realm when operating in this Gift.

-This Gift shows the angelic realm and assists us to work with those angels commissioned to aid us, protect, and minister to us and work with us. There are numerous references of angel assistance as God commanded the angels to assist us. Hebrews 1:13-14 "But to which of the angels has He ever said: 'Sit at My right hand, till I make Your enemies Your footstool.' Are they not all ministering spirits sent forth to minister for those who will inherit salvation?" Dealing with angels takes special wisdom as they work from a different vantage point than we do. Also, remember they are holy and require respectful interaction from us. Taking the time to pause and prepare for the interaction when it happens will bring us to a focused in-the-moment place, so we can respond and interact correctly. Luke 1:29-39 shows Mary's encounter with Gabriel and illustrates this brilliantly.

-Reveal what the heavenly realm is flowing in to help the church move to where God is.

-It reveals what kind of spirit is working through a person (angels or ungodly spirits) and combined with the other two gifts, shows what method to use for deliverance, healing, and counselling. Acts 16:16 & 18 "Now it happened, as we went to prayer that a certain slave girl possessed with a spirit of divination met us, who brought her masters much profit by fortune-telling... And this she did for many days. But Paul, greatly annoyed, turned and said to the spirit, 'I command you in the name of Jesus Christ to come out of her.' And he came out that very hour." It's also used in cognitive counselling to reveal core beliefs that have roots in ancestral and other bondages.

-This Gift is used in the different approaches taken in deliverance to establish which is the correct way to handle the situation. Is the person controlled, oppressed or tormented by the spirit? Is the spirit in, on or controlling the person? All deliverance must have counselling before and after to ensure that the clean 'house' of the person is filled with God, leaving no room for that spirit to return and enabling the person to grow in an area previously bound and unfruitful. Matthew 9:42 "And as he was still coming, the demon threw him down and convulsed him. Then Jesus rebuked the unclean spirit, healed the child, and gave him back to his father."

-In ministering, it reveals through sight, vision or impression specific information about a spirit and how that information should be used to achieve the Spirit directed result. Reveals what the heavenly realm is flowing in to help the church move to where God is. It reveals the third heaven and the work of the holy angels and the prophetic future already sealed and now being outworked in time and space, here on earth. The revelation of the exalted Christ, the throne of God, the Seven Spirits of the Holy Spirit, angelic beings of all levels and types and holy elders. It opens up the heavenly realm and shows the beauty of our final destination. Revelation 4:1-2 "After these things I looked, and behold, a door standing open in heaven. And the first voice which I heard was like a trumpet speaking with me, saying, 'Come up here, and I will show you things which must take place after this.' Immediately I was in the Spirit; and behold, a throne set in heaven, and One sat on the throne."

As with all good gifts, we have the choice to obey the manifestation of the revelation or not or obey in part. The full scope of all time and all spiritual truths that God knows can be revealed in these three revelational gifts. The Spirit decides the amount, depth, and limit to what is revealed according to His purposes.

Inspirational Gifts. These Gifts inspire, propel, motivate, change the individual or church. The Inspirational Gifts inspire people through worship, such as Song of the Lord, and in foretelling and forthtelling. Instruction, edification, correction, rebuke, comfort and exhortation can manifest through tongues, interpretation or prophecy.

-These gifts use speech to manifest the direct revelation of the presence of God. All three are used to teach and direct the people or person in the will of God for the present or in things to come.

-All three Gifts use instruction, edification, correction, comfort, and exhortation

-These Gifts are present when the church or individual has suffered or changed direction and bring healing, assurance, strength, and comfort. Counselling is empowered by these Gifts as is pastoral care, teaching and the prophetic ministries.

The three Inspirational gifts.

▪**Prophecy.** An utterance in a known tongue or an action or gesture or illustration or song that conveys the mind of God, the intent of God, the judgment of God, the thought of God. It can take several forms to drive a point home. Prophecy is the Spirit speaking through a believer in their own tongue, while tongues is the same operation, only not in the native language of the speaker. When prophecy is spoken it can be as forthtelling or foretelling, exhortation, comfort, edification, warning, judgment or pronouncement. With music it can take on the Song of the Lord, our prophetic response to the Song of the Lord and prophetic worship. Prophetic prayer and prophetic warfare usually combine actions or gestures, words and song or music. -

-Most prevalent in practice in the Body of Christ is the prophetic that deals with edification, exhortation and comfort. However, the New Testament is not exclusively these three manifestations. 1 Corinthians 14:3 "But he who prophesies speaks edification and exhortation and comfort to men." It's prevalent because it's taught as the only three manifestations of prophecy in the New Testament church. Although we are under grace and all the gifts are anointed within that grace, all the gifts of the Holy Spirit that operated in certain manifestations in the Old Testament operate in the same and extended manifestations within the Body of Christ. It's important to keep context of the entire message Paul was teaching on prophecy, so we must read the above in context.

-1 Corinthians 14:24-25 shows this Gift used so that the unbeliever is convinced, judged, or will have the secrets of his heart revealed and become so convinced and overcome by the fear of the Lord as to fall down in worship. This is followed by the ascension gifts coming alongside this person to bring them clarity of what they experienced. This is the prophetic working beyond the exhortation, edification and comfort in a gathering where unbelievers are present, and the Gift is working specifically for the unbelievers. This level of the Gift flows through seasoned, accurate prophets. 1 Corinthians 14:29-32 "Let two or three prophets speak, and let the others judge. But if anything is revealed to another who sits by, let the first keep silent. For you can all prophesy one by one, that all may learn and all may be encouraged. And the spirits of the prophets are subject to the prophets." The prophets spoken of in 1 Corinthians 14 operate in the office of a prophet given in ascension gifts and has depth of knowledge and understanding of God's heart and mind and is God's mouthpiece to the church.

-1 Corinthians 14:29-32 All prophecy must be judged. Paul shows a clear progression of the prophetic and the level of gifting in this chapter and Romans 12. The motivational gifts which include prophecy, operate by grace through our faith and are different from the Gift the Spirit gives as He wills. All forms of prophecy and prophetic utterance should be given free reign as there is learning and encouragement through prophecy for the church. Otherwise we are quenching the

Holy Spirit by dictating He may only address us through edification, exhortation or comfort.

-Where the Holy Spirit releases the Gifts and prophecy comes forth, we find that in people with prophetic giftings that edification, exhortation, and comfort will come forth in greater depth than the motivational gifts which function by faith.

▪**Divers Tongues.** We've looked at tongues and we have seen that tongues are a manifestation of the Spirit without measure.

-Divers tongues simply mean different tongues, and in the church setting, always has interpretation with it to ensure there is a building up of the church. The only exception is when it is for the benefit of unbelievers, and these are not unknown tongues but real languages as happened on the day of Pentecost. Acts 2:1-21.

-Tongues given in succession don't have to be the same content but they will usually follow the same theme or build on one another in different directions for one picture. The foundation of this tongue or any spiritual gift is love. It must be done in love and for the edification of the Body of Christ. Interpretation is present.

-Angelic tongues are known languages, that is why Paul states 'tongues of angels and men', indicating it is a learned language not an unknown tongue. However, these may manifest in church, but they are not a Gift of the Spirit.

-The Baptism of the Holy Spirit results in a more free-flowing of manifestations, the first usually is speaking in an unknown tongue. It 'charges up' and gets us in the flow that allows the Gift to work fully within the church and in conjunction with the other gifts given by God.

•**Interpretation of Tongues.** This gift is the only of the Gifts that must have another of the Gifts to operate.

-Although all the Gifts interweave, they are all able to stand alone except this and the previous one. Divers Tongues and Interpretation of Tongues are gifts given to the Body of believers and significantly the only two gifts that must co-operate and harmonize to be effective in a church setting!

-Interpretation of tongues is not translation of the words uttered in the tongue, it's usually the content of the meaning that was uttered not the exact translation of the words. That is why a tongue given may be longer or shorter than the interpretation.

-Interpretation can come in the form of a description of a picture received during the tongue, a phrase, an idea or a set of words. Only one interpretation of a tongue is permitted 1 Corinthians 14:27 to prevent disorder and keep this from overtaking the service.

-Interpretation may take on a different tone in the voice of the one interpreting, it may become sing song, soft, loud or uncharacteristically different. 1 Corinthians 14:4-5 & 12-40.

-We can pray and ask to have interpretation of our private tongue given. One way to train ourselves to be open to interpretation of our private tongue is to pray in our known language in our minds while praying in our unknown tongue vocally. As tongues don't require our mental ability we can focus on our mind's prayer. Initially there is an awareness that two different prayers are being prayed but then there will be times where it's clear you are thinking or 'praying' the interpretation mentally. It's also a great way to stop our minds from wandering during our heavenly tongue praying. This interpretation doesn't happen all the time, as private tongues must serve as edification and receiving of mysteries primarily.

However, we can train ourselves to sensitize even more in this precious Gift by following the above. As the Spirit wills, He then has us available when He wants to flow through us in this manner and train us for corporate worship interpretation.

Here are the ground rules of how corporate operation of vocal gifts should function. Firstly, all things must be for edification, for the building up of the Body of Christ corporately. Hence if tongues are shared publicly, each should have a turn to speak and each tongue should be interpreted. The emphasis is on order, so that the church is edified.

Weigh the word received to see if it will edify the Body, if not discuss it privately with leadership. Wrong words or wrong timing of words can quench the Spirit during our time with God. When the Spirit chooses, several people may get interlinking messages. The emphasis is on order, so that the church is edified. 1 Corinthians 14:5 "I wish you all spoke with tongues, but even more that you prophesied; for he who prophesies is greater than he who speaks with tongues, unless indeed he interprets, that the church may receive edification."

Power Gifts. These gifts manifest in tangible means to reveal God and intervene and change the natural order of things by superimposing the divine on the natural. The fullness of eternal heaven and the Presence of God breaks through. All nine Gifts can be used by God to bring deliverance but these three manifestly and evidently destroy the works of the enemy and the marring effects of wrong thinking and living in quantifiable measures.

-Any natural event or circumstance that is suddenly reversed into something different, opposite, or greater. It's a definite, clear change that is evident to our senses.

-The power Gifts take no extra effort or increased faith

because like the other Gifts, they are given as the Spirit sees the need for that Gift to be manifested. A willingness and obedience in Spirit led living increases the opportunities that we may be used.

-These Gifts often combine other Gifts, as in the case in 2 Kings 5 where the prophet Elisha tells Naaman to go wash seven times in the Jordan and when he finally does, he is instantly healed.

▪Gift of Faith. This is the supernatural Gift of Faith that allows us to believe the impossible and see it manifest. (It's not the measure of faith received so we can be saved, nor is it the faith we develop throughout our lives.)

-The Gift of faith is released for a time for a specific task and a tangible and manifest turnabout is usually seen in a very short space of time. Jesus told the fig tree to die and fully accepted that it was dead immediately. Matthew 21:19-21

-The Gift usually comes on us suddenly and without even realizing it, we operate in it. This is not staying the course in faith but more like a 'faith assignment' with an objective, a target and a time limit.

-This Gift takes our knowing or seeing the objective and spontaneously flows out from the revelation of what the Holy Spirit has given. It's a quick response to the prompting that releases this Gift, but if we lose the vision the Gift may stop working. See Peter walking on water as the perfect example. Matthew 14:28-29.

-The Gift of faith will manifest in conjunction with the Gifts of healings or the working of miracles, but it can also function completely independently of any other Gift.

-This Gift often works with prophecy as with Elisha in 2

Kings 7 and word of knowledge. Elisha knew it was done the moment he told the king.

-The Gift of Faith operates on the heart assurance that it will come to pass. In 1 Kings 17:13-16 Elijah, after a revelation from God, finds a widow woman to sustain him. She is almost out of food and he tells her to make him a cake first and then feed herself and her son, promising that the meal or oil would not end.

-This Gift stops the moment the thing comes to pass.

■**Gift of Healings.** As the plurality of the name suggests, many types of manifestation of healing are wrapped up in the Gift of Healings. A broad definition would include repair, cure, make whole, heal or deliver the body, mind, spirit, or social and financial realms, bondage in ancestral problems, sickness, disease or trauma. Healing of water (2 Kings 2:21-22), land, barrenness in land or womb, plagues and pestilences are all shown to yield to the Holy Spirit's Gifts of healings. It may also represent healing of a particular ailment repeatedly by an individual such as repeatedly praying for cancer effectively or for knee joints repeatedly. Matthew 8:13-16.

-Very often those who have been miraculously healed of a life threatening or serious disease will be imbued by the Spirit to administer healing in the same area for others by the laying on of hands. This is partly due to the fact of the conviction of God's healing power born through the miracle in the one healed. It's also partly because the Holy Spirit works in the economy of God by utilizing every testimony to multiply itself. In other words, we are healed to be used in the healing others. Acts 9:17-18.

-The Gift of Healings often but not always require touch (Acts 3:1-10) or an action that must be performed to gain end result. Due to the flow of healing power it is seldom necessary to directly touch the area requiring healing. Acts 9:32-35.

-The Gift of Healings are often combined with other gifts to make preaching more effective, as in Acts 8:6-7 "all gave heed to the words he spoke."

-The Gift of Healings are used to deliver from spiritual oppression and heal those who are sick or bound through trauma. Acts 10:38 It will work in conjunction with other Gifts such as discernment of spirits, prophecy etc.

-Gift of Healings can work through the touch of the shadow of the person imbued or objects imbued by one through laying on of hands, for example. This gift can be transferred to materials or be released through the shadow or proximity of the person. Acts 5:15-16. It can also work remotely without any contact. Matthew 8:13.

-Several points are apparent from Acts 3:3-8 that are often present: Peter sought eye contact and held his attention, then he issued a short faith command, he followed it with a gesture and contact point and the man immediately was completely healed, as Peter expected.

▪**Working of Miracles.** God suspends or supersedes natural laws with the spiritual to further His plans and purposes and to bear witness of Himself and His kingdom. Hebrews 2:4. It confirms the Word of God. John 10:25.

-Working of Miracles is a sign of God's Presence. For instance, when God called Gideon, Gideon asked God, "If I am a mighty man of valour where are all the miracles?" This was why Moses asked God to be with him to perform miracles. This is why Elisha asked, "Where is the Lord God of Elijah?"

-It causes astonishment, wonder and deep reflection on the nature of God and brings the person to a place of encountering and having to deal with a very real manifestation of God. Hebrews 2:3.

-The raising of the dead is usually the Working of Miracles. Acts 9:37-40.

-The transmutation of one substance to another totally unrelated substance, restore what has decomposed, as in the case of Lazarus, instantaneous regeneration of limbs or organs, on and on.

-This Gift is used to increase or change or purify foods. Read this portion of scripture to see the various aspects of the Gift of working of miracles 2 Kings 4:1-44.

-Through the Gift of Working of Miracles the waters were held back Exodus 14:21-26, the sun stood still Joshua 10:13, an axe floated 2 Kings 6:5-6, the fire did not burn Daniel 3:15-26.

-Through the Gift of Working of Miracles, Jesus turned the water into wine John 2. And Jesus fed 5000 with 5 loaves and 2 fish. In this small selection of the miracles of the bible the Spirit shows God is a God of miracles.

Now with clear examples of what the Gifts do and how they work, let's look at your Gifts uniquely…

I'm Gifted!

Your unique life will have a unique flow of the Gifts through you, throughout your life. You will also have temporary empowerments at specific times.

The Gifts of the Holy Spirit empower you to walk in the reality of a deposit of the Holy Spirit. In other words, you have power to live and change things, change people and change yourself because of the Spirit within.

Growing in the Gifts.

The Gifts are life transforming and powerful and will change you, those around you and assist you in living a life of destiny. Taking time to grow and hone your ability in the Gifts. Following the advice in this and other chapters will make you a better conduit for the Holy Spirit. Paul took great care to give comprehensive teaching on all the Gifts of the Godhead and in these teachings lie the keys to help us operate with familiarity in the gifts given. (More on all the Godhead Gifts? Read 'Gifts for destiny and life'[5])

No matter how much you are already seeing of the flow of the power and presence of the Spirit, seek more! If you're flowing in tongues and interpretation, seek to grow in prophecy. Ask the Spirit to use you, surround yourself with wise teachers, listen and act on what the Spirit says. It's in the act of doing that you grow and learn more about the scope of your Gifts and yourself and grow in your relationship with God.

This is a good place to take a moment and discover more about yourself. Before reading further, print this out and answer the questions. There are no right or wrong answers, so just fill in what feels right to you.

https://thefluidway.com/wp-content/uploads/2020/08/My-

Spiritual-Gifts-Profile-1.pdf

2 Corinthians 3:3 "You are manifestly an epistle of Christ, ministered by us, written not with ink but by the Spirit of the living God, not on tablets of stone but on tablets of flesh, that is, of the heart."

Being familiar with your own unique mental and spiritual 'wiring' gives you the ability to explore how you can co-operate within these Gifts in your life to be effective in releasing and living in kingdom power and destiny. As the Gifts and the Fruit blend to create a balanced life of power and wholeness, take a break here and allow yourself some quiet time to think and pray about what you discovered in your Spiritual Gifts Profile and what that means.

Once you've done this and you understand more about your blend of Gifts, let's then turn our attention to the Fruit of the Spirit...

LET'S TALK ABOUT LOVE

"God is love." 1 John 4:8

In looking at love, the best place to start is at the source of love: God. Everything we have as kingdom dwellers is as a result of God's love. God doesn't love, He is love and His love is dynamic. What does that mean? **This is not some fuzzy feeling, but the very energy emanating from God as part of Him that caused creation and redemption. This energy produces, it creates, and is dynamic.** This is the love that is referred to as the manifestation of the Fruit of the Spirit from which all other manifestations emanate.

God-love is beautifully expressed in John 3:16 "God so loved the world He gave His only begotten Son, that whoever believes in Him should not perish but have everlasting life."

We see that this energy called love that is God doing five distinct things:

-God's love is not selective, it's available to anyone.
-God loved and created - He gave of Himself.
-God's love continues for His creation and He gives His very best and most precious gift, His only Son.
-God's love secures and centres us in Him and His

kingdom eternally.
-God's love is dynamic and it has perpetual and lasting results.

This is the very heart of real love and the foundation that the Fruit rests on and all the wholeness of the Spirit flows from. **This pure energy called love flows everywhere and you can flow with it and allow it to flow through you.** By doing this, you surrender your life to the love that is God and release the power of that love to produce and create through you and in you.

1 John 4:16."And we have known and believed the love God has for us. God is love, and he who abides in love abides in God, and God in him." Wow! By living in this love you are centred in God. **Love is an energy source of all heaven and all of that is available to you every day for your life and through you to the world.**

It's in this love we find God and this is where we experience all His doings because love and God cannot be separated. This love energy infuses and transforms what it touches – if we allow it. In encountering this God-love we have a response, whether subtle or blatant, accepting or rejecting. We make micro decisions every day about how we will respond to this love in our lives and relationships and how we will act as a result of our choice.

When we "abide in love" we are "abiding in God" – there is an awareness in abiding. **You live in the centre of a powerful, pure energy that is God's, but this energy will only fully express itself in your life if you have the intent of God.** And God's intent is summed up in the five distinct things that is revealed in John 3:16. By using the wrong intent, (Luke 9:55), what you are sowing has consequences in what you reap, Galatians 6:7. This applies in every area of your life and that is why I stressed how important it is to examine and grow in your inner life. In Luke 9:55, the disciples used truth but in skewed thinking and that's why Jesus rebuked them – their intent, their heart power, was deflected through wrong emotional response to a situation. Love was not the foundation to their actions. Intent is powerful, it fuels your desires, so we'll look at it fully later in this book.

Love powerfully demonstrates God's intent.

God-love is not a feeling or relationship based on common interests, instead, it's propelled by the highest interests beyond feeling. **It's loving and giving the very best for the pure sake of loving and giving, whether the receiver is worthy or not.** God demonstrates this by allowing us to come to Him, as we are, at salvation. **His love response is fuelled by our need.** There is great passion and desire to touch, to reach and to meet our need and then go beyond that abundantly.

God-love knows no bounds in expression and is limitless in pursuit to shower this love upon another. **God is love, so everything about Him and from Him flows through that pure love energy.** This is available to anyone at any time, all they have to do is come to Him and establish relationship with Him. That's it.

There are no conditions to have access to God-love for anyone alive. The whole earth feels God's love through creation, His laws placed lovingly in nature, His gift of our minds and abilities to create etc. **There is evidence all around us of the love of God.** He continually expresses His love by the pursuing power that never gives up until restoration or death finalizes the choice of the one pursued. **However, to experience all and understand and fully**

flow in this love we need to be in the kingdom. He constantly shows Himself to all and calls all home to a kingdom life, 1 Thessalonians 2:12 "God who calls you into His own kingdom and glory." It's up to us to take what's offered.

And it is in the kingdom that we find full expression of our lives, our purpose for being. **Being created in love and by love, we only truly thrive in the kingdom when we fully assume God's nature and perspective and operate from His intent.** We live in the Fruit to be fully fruitful. The kingdom is saturated in God-love, so, operating from this dynamic place, we become loving creators, building our Father's kingdom.

But we live in the world filled with many things contrary to love and light. Because we are in the world but not of it, we take hold of 1 John 4:17 "Love has been perfected among us...because as He is so are we in this world." That all-pervading God-love is perfected in us through the perspective change that came through redemption and kingdom living. Yet surrounded by many things that do not reflect that love, we access the empowering of the Fruit and mental abilities we have to help us grow. **We intentionally use our life to create a place for the God-love to flow through and become a contact point to others. That requires taking on God's way of thinking.**

Maximum impact through ultimate giving.

When we needed to be rescued from our own skewed thinking and doing, God's plan involved giving all of Him, His very most, His very best, and His only Son. **This is God's thinking operating in love.** Redemption is an extravagant thing. It's not a little prayer and a change of mind. He decided to enter the time tunnel to speak to us face to face, to love us and point the way back to kingdom living. He lived and died like any human to express His understanding and affinity with our human existence. And at the moment of your restored relationship with God, His very life giving Spirit entered your life and overcame the spirit of death and transformed you utterly to a being of light and life. As you enter the kingdom, He reveals Himself, His treasures, His wisdom and His power to you and encourages you to take what you want to use in your life. He delights in you, spends time with you to listen and talk to you, protects you, enriches you, heals you, empowers you and guides you. And to make sure you know He is always close, His very own Spirit is with you. **God's love intentionally surrounds and saturates your life abundantly and this love brings about all the blessings of the kingdom.**

Paul urges, "Let this mind be in you that was also in Christ Jesus." Philippians 2:5. Jesus, God's very best and only Son, took on flesh with a mission: He came to express God's love. So this is the mental 'place', the perspective of God we live in and express to the world. And, like Jesus, we demonstrate before we talk about love. We often hear the term 'walk in love' in the church but in order to do that we must have the right perspective – a kingdom mentality. **It's understanding the pure power of love and ensuring you do what it takes to create the thinking and intentions that match God's intentions and thinking. You train your thinking to copy Jesus.**

Jesus expressed God's love in His actions – He lived love. So, having the right intention, the right 'heart place' in any matter must then be followed by the expression of that love in action. One of the five things we found in John 3:16 is that God's love is dynamic: there is action that produces results.

Love creates.

This pure love energy that is God contains His dynamic nature. God is creative and when He speaks things form and become. Hebrews 11:3. He created a creation that was "very good". **Love flows through God's dynamic nature, so all the power of love is evident in all dynamic creation.** All of creation at its core is infused with God-love, the "very good" of Genesis 1, and Jesus came to restore that. He destroyed the 'gunk' that tarnished that pure love infused in creation so it's accessible and evident to all. Giving the best, restoring it when it was tarnished by us and now maintaining it as our kingdom living.

Here's an example of God-love to you: Psalm 103:2-5 "Bless the Lord, O my soul, And forget not all His benefits; Who forgives all your iniquities, Who heals all your diseases, Who redeems your life from destruction, Who crowns you with lovingkindness and tender mercies, Who satisfies your mouth with good things, So that your youth is renewed like the eagle's." So you see God's love encompasses every area of your life, everything, and brings benefit to every area by increasing and improving and healing and loving kindness. God-love in action, loving and giving.

Every creative act is founded in love. This is how God loves. This love gives because it loves. **It not only gives, but it also gives the most, the best. It gives all in pursuit of showering this love.** We can only love like this through thinking and acting like Jesus. God-love is only possible in the redeemed and surrendered life under the direction of the Spirit manifested Fruit and by aligning and training your mind with the thinking of God.

Thinking like God.

Ephesians 3:15-19 "…from whom the whole family in heaven and earth is named, that He would grant you…to be strengthened with might through His Spirit in the inner man…that you, being rooted and grounded in love…know the love of Christ which passes knowledge; that you may be filled with all the fullness of God." The very honesty of God-love is a thing of soul-shivering wonder. It is what it is, with no hidden agenda, no small print, no disclaimer. God's love is available to anyone and His Spirit gives to His creation continuously, keeping us secure and centred in Him and His kingdom eternally. His dynamic love has perpetual and lasting results in our lives here and the life to come. This is the unchanging truth declared in Malachi 3:6 "For I am the Lord, I do not change." It's a truth we base our lives on because we know it's the reality of who God is and who we are in Him.

The Real Deal

Loving by being real.

In Exodus 3:14 God declares, …I AM WHO I AM…Thus you shall say to the children of Israel, 'I AM has sent me to you.'" I AM WHO I AM is more than God stating He is God, it's God's declaration of His eternal authenticity. It's a guaranteed 'you can take this to the bank' type statement. Nothing needed to be added – God is God, He is true and it will happen because God-love is in action.

God demonstrates His love through His authenticity in every action. **Why is this so important? Because you've got to be real, authentic, in your intent if you want the pure, desired result.** God always gets the desired result because His intent is always authentic. He confirms it over and over. Hebrews 11:6 "…for he who comes to God must believe He is, and that He is a rewarder of those who diligently seek Him."

Authentically me.

Being real in the presence of God is the foundation of your relationship with Him. From the moment you came to Him at salvation you've had to step deeper and deeper into your authentic self. Your love relationship with God compels honesty. Your mind renewal, changing your behaviour, learning to operate in the Spirit with the mind of Christ and every other step of growth you've taken as a believer required you to be real. You had to face yourself and hold it to the truth of the kingdom and then make the adjustments necessary.

The kingdom and kingdom living is profoundly real and powerful.

As a believer in the kingdom you can only experience all of the kingdom from the place of truth. If you, for example, refuse to renew your mind and that part of you stays in old thinking and doing, you can't walk in the light or the full power of the light. God places great store in you being real and living authentically. **Authenticity is your way of celebrating the uniqueness God placed in you.** Being real and true to all of what's inside. That includes the parts you like and the parts you don't, that you tend to hide away from everyone else. This is where the material we've covered in this book will help move beyond what was to what God lovingly planned for you, uniquely, when He called you into existence. But how does being authentic fit in with love?

Jesus sets the scene.

We have an awesome story in the bible where Jesus gives a

profound and life changing teaching on being real and living an authentic life. In the midst of yet another pressing day of ministry, Jesus goes and sits at a well. He strikes up a conversation with a woman who comes to draw water. In their ensuing conversation, Jesus reveals she has had 5 husbands and is currently living with a man. The truth of this is acknowledged by her when she calls Him a prophet while discussing her take on doctrine. But He's not just talking about our formal worship, He had purposely steered the conversation to include her living arrangement because He wants to address her living authentically. Let's see what happened next.

John 4:24-26 "'God is Spirit, and those who worship Him must worship Him in spirit and truth'. The woman said to Him, 'I know that Messiah is coming' (who is called Christ). 'When He comes, He will tell us all things.' Jesus said to her, "I who speak to you am He.'"

'Worship' comes from the word 'to kiss', it's face-to-face in the most intimate form of love. Nothing is hidden. No wonder the word for 'truth' used here is 'not concealing'! **Jesus uses these words purposely to show that if we are concealing, we are not worshipping in spirit and truth.** So, we not only disconnect ourselves from God, but we also disconnect ourselves from the power of our redeemed spirit if we insist on not being real.

Instead of focusing on her physical state of wrong, Jesus offers her life and brings her to the core of her need for transformation, releasing her potential to live a life of authenticity. Through her subsequent testimony, many from her town believed.

Authenticity causes a reaction: people sit up and take note.

It stirs desire in those who encounter it to pursue it and have that revealed in them. We, as the Body, become the example and the advertisement of what is possible, and desire is stirred in those who don't know Him for an encounter that will transform them. Through this, His Body, the church, grows.

The more we repair ourselves as image bearers of God, the less concealment we need.

1 John 1:5-7 "… God is light and in Him is no darkness at all. If we say that we have fellowship with Him, and walk in darkness, we lie and do not practise the truth. But if we walk in the light as He is in the light, we have fellowship with one another, and the blood of Jesus Christ His Son cleanses us from all wrong." The power of walking in light as the real you is you have constant access to the renewal and cleansing power of God to continue your unfolding glory in Christ. Living in untarnished love and light.

Darkness is that state devoid of light and of God. The word 'darkness' in the scripture above means, 'obscurity' which in turn is defined as 'devoid of light, hidden'. It follows therefore that any part of us that remains hidden or devoid of the light of God does not operate in the sameness of God re-established through redemption. It remains in obscurity. **That part cannot look or act like God nor will it yield to the plan of God.** It's contrary in nature and make up and has opposite goals to God. How will the Spirit of truth residing in us inhabit the hidden part yielded to untruth? God cannot touch or change any un-surrendered part of us we keep in isolation. He never violates our free will.

Finding and releasing your authentic self.

Psalm 33:11 & 15 "The counsel of the Lord stands

87

forever, the plans of His heart to all generations…He fashions their heart individually; He considers all their works." You are uniquely made and living authentically enables you 'to worship (and relate) in spirit and in truth'. It starts by being truthful with yourself and being willing to go to God to reveal where you need to bring authenticity to your life.

When you know that you're operating in the truth of yourself, your emotions and your destiny without compromise to God, you're living in the zone. **There's a flow and peace and ease that passes what we normally know and live in.** The Fruit can flow and nothing restricts your access to God and His goodness.

By looking at your inner world, your thoughts and the stories you live, you can expose what is not real and true and change it. Philippians 4:8 "Finally, brethren, whatever things are true, whatever things are noble, whatever things are just, whatever things are pure, whatever things are lovely, whatever things are of good report, if there is any virtue and if there is anything praiseworthy - meditate on these things." Keeping our minds on the things of God and seeking to walk in the Spirit, we don't allow the flesh to rule. Our spirit remains open to the leading and direction of the Holy Spirit and the manifestation of the Fruit of the Spirit flows through the yielded spirit. **But the above scripture also needs to be applied to whatever things you think about yourself: you should focus on the true, noble, just, pure, lovely, good reports, and all things of virtue about yourself.** This starts in knowing and loving ourselves. But all this is only possible if we allow ourselves to be real.

Loving God and loving others as ourselves requires us to know and understand how to God-love ourselves.

The Fruit of the Spirit is there for you to operate in love to yourself as well. You can't love your neighbour as yourself if you don't love yourself. That's a given. Many people struggle finding a balance between loving yourself and being self-involved. Using the blueprint of God-love you would:

-love and cherish the body that houses you and is your vehicle to destiny living. You would treat it as a living, amazing organism by looking after it, loving it and protecting it. **I intentionally bless my body and tell it that I love it and thank it daily for functioning perfectly and giving me such an amazing 'house' to live in. I follow my intentioned gratitude by listening to my body and caring for it in the best possible way.**

1 Corinthians 6:19 "...your body is the temple of the Holy Spirit, who is in you, whom you have from God, and you are not your own." This does not only mean that you house the Spirit of the very living God, but that God, in effect, expresses and lives through your life. Remove the religious aspect of this and see it for what it is: **Your body is inhabited by God-love.**

-grow your awareness of yourself and the 'dimensions' of your life. Explore and delight in your inner world and the mental and emotional abilities you have and find ways to maximize them by lovingly growing your mind and self. You would remove things that harm you or lessen your mind or your life and be protective of what you allow in your mind and life. **By simply having the perspective of God-love for yourself you will live, flow and grow your life in the dynamic power of God.**

-be able to live from an overflowing of God-love that radiates out and expands into every encounter and action in your relating in the world. **Living inside God-love becomes the**

default setting of your life. Now you can operate like God.

So, right here and now, take a moment to think about how you love yourself. Each of us interact with ourselves differently. Are there areas you need to change how you treat yourself? Take time to write them down while they are fresh in your mind. (Writing something down on paper using a pen is tactile and makes it real). Now look at these areas. How are they hurting or limiting you in view of what you know through this book? Write that down. Take a moment to pray how to change this and then listen to what the Spirit says. Then take a few moments and allow your amazing brain to work on a solution for you by asking yourself with intension 'How do I change (whatever you wrote down) to express God-love for myself? Deal with each area you found separately and ask the question for each area and write down your answer. Once you've done that ask, 'How would I act and be different?' Write that down. **It's not just about knowing where you should change the way you love yourself but also about finding ways to change that and incorporating them in your life daily.** Now include it in your daily quiet time with God so you can establish it as a lifestyle and grow in your love for yourself in a healthy, Fruit-filled manner.

Create in love.

When we operate in our desires to create a good life from the Fruit of love, we access the pure love energy of God Himself and we can create from a point of love. What does this mean? The spiritual laws that govern intentioned creation and sowing and reaping work through the Golden Rule: What you do unto others will be done to you. If you simply look after yourself and your emphasis is for your gain regardless of others, you cannot fully access the dynamic power of God's abundance. But if your whole attitude to creating your good life is to benefit and create an environment of abundance for others, you work through the pure energy of God-love in creating. To illustrate, it's like the declaration from someone saying they will begin to help others in need, and give a huge amount to help others as soon as they've made their fortune. That very thinking shows the starting point and the intent is selfish and not God-love based. God-love working in us motivates us to do good with our resources even when we have little.

Look again at God's intent reflected in the five things that John 3:16 taught us at the beginning of the chapter. Real love is dynamic and flows outward unconditionally. **It works in your life when you operate from the kingdom perspective that you are a conduit for this love to flow in and through.** All your intentioned actions and thinking then take on the real and generous dynamic nature of God.

Love has fruit.

Because God-love is more a response than a feeling, it's not tied to circumstances and is evident regardless of what is going on. **This love always shows – it's demonstrative, so it always has fruit or results.** God wants you to multiply, be prosperous, have a healthy, happy and abundant life. It's up to you to cultivate the right kingdom mentality and operate in the foundations laid by the Fruit of the Spirit. This pleases God. So how do we begin to cultivate living in this kind of love? By looking at how we can express this God-love. 1 Corinthians 13:4-8 "Love suffers long and is kind; love does not envy; love does not parade itself, is not puffed up; does not behave rudely, does not seek its own, is not provoked, thinks no evil; does not rejoice in iniquity, but rejoices in the truth; bears all things, believes all things, hopes all things, endures all things. Love never fails."

This encapsulation of love folds in every other manifestation of the Fruit. It has identifiable characteristics: 1 Corinthians 13 clearly is the God-love chapter. Every time the words 'love' or 'charity' are mentioned it's God-love. Notice the progression in 1 Corinthians. Paul speaks of the unity in diversity of spiritual gifts in 1 Corinthians 12 and continues with the nine Gifts of the Holy Spirit in 1 Corinthians 14. Sandwiched in the middle of the operation of the Gifts, we have an entire chapter dealing with God-love. Why? **Gifts must express love through authentic intent!**

Let's break down the thinking we cultivate and the actions our thinking produces when we act in love.

-Longsuffering or patient in relating to others. Approaching our dealings with others in the understanding that they are wired differently, are dealing with their own inner world on their own journey through life. We understand that every person is growing at their own rate and we let them do that. We don't impose conditions to loving them or blessing them. And by not setting an agenda to our love, we don't get disappointed or frustrated when they choose to behave or relate in dysfunction.

Being longsuffering or patient does not mean you stay in abusive relationships. Your body is a temple of the Holy Spirit. Your God-love for yourself enables you to think how you will relate and, in some circumstances, when to walk away from that relationship. This allows them to face themselves, not in relation to the relationship but in relation to their behaviour.

Both longsuffering and patience requires you to find intelligent ways in your relating. If you don't have an answer and you are unsure how to operate in the Fruit in a situation, seek a good counsellor to give you the psychological tools.

-Kindness is showing oneself as useful and acting benevolently. Manifesting active God-love on behalf of those who have need. Cultivating an awareness of the world around us and actively seeking to do acts of kindness every day, just as God does. (More later).

-Living without envy means you are zealous of others' good fortune and delight in the good fortune of others. It's a state of mind that allows us to pray blessing over everyone, even those who are spiteful or hurtful toward us. This is the best way to prevent that hurt from growing in your life to become a limiting belief or a root of bitterness.

Envy comes from the perspective that someone has something I should have or deserve. Do you see that's the wrong perspective? Think for a moment what kind of feelings you experienced and what you thought when you felt envy. If you accept your kingdom heritage then everything is yours, you just may not have it...YET. By changing your perspective when you feel envy to 'I don't have that...yet', you open a way for you to pray about it and then ask your amazing brain what action would bring you to the point where you CAN have it.

Praying blessings over those more fortunate sets us free from the bondage of desiring another's good fortune and releases us to focus on what God has destined for us. It also 'unblocks' the areas of envy or frustration that may have developed so that the pure power of God can flow through us into our life.

-Boasting comes from an insecurity that we and our lives are not enough and is usually motivated by a deep need for recognition. Limiting core beliefs we hold about ourselves as a result of what we believe about ourselves prevent us thinking and living with a kingdom mentality. Understanding and living what we have already covered in this book, you are growing in what you have as joint-heir with Christ. Focus on building your life and destiny and let your fruit speak for your life. Matthew 7:16 "You will know them by their fruits." This attitude will liberate us from desiring the approval of others and we can focus our effort instead on pleasing God and fulfilling our destiny.

Boasting does not have real creative power. When you use your words to speak intentionally from God-love, all of God's dynamic power is available to you to create. But because boasting starts from an illusion of what is real, it doesn't have the substance of God behind it. Remember, God is always authentic and so are you as a joint-heir with Christ. **So, create a strong personal brand that will promote you on the evidence of your life because there is nothing wrong with promoting yourself if it's done right.**

-Pride can take on many forms and I won't deal with that. Instead I want to focus back on God's thinking and how we can copy it. We seek to find and release the gifts and callings in others to raise them to the place of destiny. Express pride in others and what they are and do. That is such a great motivation to others and will encourage them. Always be approachable by all around and try and find common ground to relate. If you can promote a deserving person, do so. Use your sphere of influence, your abilities and your powers to make it happen. Don't seek a payback, just do it because you can.

You should be proud of achievements like finishing a degree, being successful in business or whatever else, it's normal to feel pleasure in your achievements but success should never change your character or your attitude to others.

-Behaving rudely is focused on self at the disregard of all else and shows discordance and discourteousness. We seek to behave in all things with grace and breeding befitting an heir of the King, ever aware that we are the fragrance of Christ to the world, observed and judged by those who are lost. The best defence against rudeness is to learn the art of being fully present in your interactions, giving people your attention and time when you are interacting by being fully 'there.'

-Self-seeking is loving with an agenda and making our relationships transactional (there must be a gain for me in the relationship) rather than transformational (we'll both grow because of the relationship). Self-seeking always revolves around self, with the entire world revolving around this person's life, comforts, ministry, or family which is contrary to everything redeemed living stands for. By staying centred in the Fruit of the Spirit we operate in God-love which will always balance our relationships in love and prevent dysfunctional relating.

-Being even-tempered and not allowing yourself to anger easily can at times be hard when you're passionate about something. Psalm 145:8 shows God's mercy and His graciousness. We cannot be rich in love and quick to anger at the same time. The word for 'provoked' comes from the word 'to stir up' and includes anything we allow to stir up in us those emotions etc. that are going to lead to unthinking reactions. By disconnecting from the stirring up and putting distance between the situation, we can step back and assess the situation from the place of 'what would Jesus do?' A good way to develop this is to have the perception of 'get the big picture.'

We can't excuse ourselves and say it's because we're passionate or it's just our nature and we're prone to anger. Anger manages things badly. Your body floods with chemicals, your posture changes, your chin pushes out, slowing oxygen flow to the brain which influences your rational thinking. And you are talking and acting while in this state of not 'thinking right'. Words have power, especially if they have passion and emotion behind them – they become intentions that create!

If you find yourself here, force yourself to stop. Take 5 deep, slow breaths. If that is not enough, take a time out by walking away from the situation and praying. Then ask yourself, 'Am I operating in God-love in a manner that is the fragrance of Christ?' 2 Corinthians 2:14 "…God who always leads us in triumph in Christ, and through us diffuses the fragrance of His knowledge in every place."

Don't repress anger when it is needed in a situation. If a gunman walks into a school and kills all the pupils, you should be angry about it. In situations like these, the emphasis is on how you direct that anger.

-Learn to be as quick to forget others' wrongdoing as God is to forget yours when you repent. Unforgiveness harboured in the heart leads to a root of bitterness that infects the spirit with hardness and invades the body with sickness. It will also affect your thinking and emotions and how you relate with people and God. Take the attitude that everyone is growing and changing and see the light in that person, focus on the light in them. Soon that will be all you'll see.

-Rejoice in good, it will help you grow a perspective that good is all around you and filling your life. Everyone including you is a work in progress, so seek to bring the best out in others and self. **Find good, spread good, do good. You are part of a kingdom saturated in good, pass it around and surround yourself with it.** In a world where you can be anything, be kind and avoid those habits, actions, and words that harm others and ultimately yourself. Actively seek to do random acts of kindness. **Bless and enhance others and the world around you, it's a tremendously satisfying place to live and will bring you a great deal of happiness.**

-Always protects in this scripture implies to cover over in silence, without exposing the faults of others. This is what is meant by love covering a multitude of sins, not in acceptance of those sins but as protection by not using things to bring further harm or shame. Jesus acted like this with the woman at the well, so you know the power that this brings in a real-life situation. When you do this you extend grace to the person to change and grow in themselves and their relationship with you.

Having an attitude of protecting also means you unconditionally protect those around you. Have a simple philosophy of not participating in something that harms another – whether in thought, action or word.

-Always trusting is an expectation that in time things will change and holding an attitude of peace with a knowing that all will work out for those submitted to God. Now this is not just sitting in a heap waiting for things to change. **Active trust has action with it. You do your part and trust because you do, God will do His part. Remember, we are dealing with God-love and God-love is dynamic.**

As with each point in this section, wisdom must be applied. For example, it's not an exercise in trust to give your wallet to someone who stole from you before! Trust in certain circumstances must be earned. In a situation like this, trust comes into the picture because you trust that once this person has developed the character to be trusted you will. Your trust is deferred but real. And you don't allow one bad thing to affect your trust level in other relationships. Just because you were robbed by one person once does not mean others will. You trust in a universal way in your life, but apply it differently to some when there are adverse circumstances.

-Hope is to expect with desire. We can do this because it is founded in God-love. This kind of hope has substance and will be the propelling force behind your faith. It's a very active, dynamic expectation with a knowing that things will change and allowing the Spirit to work in self and others. It brings with it a rest that removes the fretting and striving that can accompany plans unfolding.

Because hope is expecting with desire it fuels action in our lives. The things we hope for are backed by our faith and faith is always based in now. It's happening in this moment because we're doing and believing to make it so.

-Always persevering usually goes hand-in-hand with hope. Not giving up and focusing on the winning post and moving steadily toward your end goals regardless of circumstances. Perseverance is what will help you stick to your goals and see them through in the times when you want to give up. This is the time to dip into that ocean of God-love and find strength and renewal, and it's also a time to sit with your goals and visualise clearly what awaits you when you achieve. God-love allows us to move through life in the energy and assurance of that love. It helps us put every day and every action in perspective of destiny.

-1 Corinthians 13 ends with an absolute. "Love never fails." Love is never without effect or vain, even in the most difficult relationships and circumstances. God set the perfect example of that in Jesus, so we rest in the truth of unfailing love. Taking on this perspective helps us when in our own relationships and our self-love we struggle. **When this**

happens, re-centre yourself in that absolute truth – love never fails. Can you see how your feelings of inadequacy or unworthiness in no way lessens or impacts the reality of God's constant love?

Love is eternal.

1 Corinthians 13:8 "Love never fails. But whether there are prophecies, they will fail; whether there are tongues, they will cease; whether there is knowledge, it will vanish away." So, beyond this time in which we need the prophetic to the place of eternal future, and beyond the unifying force of unknown tongues to the place of absolute oneness with Christ eternally, this love continues.

1 Corinthians 13:13 "And now abide faith, hope, love, these three; but the greatest of these is love."

Loving others.

We all want to be loved and love and we look for it in our relationships and our lives. Applying God-love to friends, the bible gives some clear examples of the attitude and character of loving friends.

-Friends share experience and empathy: Luke 15:9 "And when she found it, she calls her friends and neighbours together, saying, 'Rejoice with me, for I have found the piece which I lost.'" The joy of one becomes joy of all. There is an intimacy in sharing the little moments that make up life.

-Esteemed friends give the one who shares an intimacy and position of honour to know and be able to act in boldness in the life of that friend. In other words, we can say things that others don't have the right to say to a friend. It's a very real, very deep relationship based on the love of that friend and wanting the best for them. This is a place earned through time and action that has proved you are safe and that my deep things are secure with you.

-Abraham had this God-love expressed as a friend of God because he adopted God's interests as his own: James 2:23 "And the Scripture was fulfilled which says, 'Abraham believed God, and it was accounted to him for righteousness.' And he was called the friend of God." His love for a Friend compelled him to accept the most painful commission of offering up his dear son as sacrifice. He did so because he understood and knew God intimately, so he knew and could trust God would not harm or hurt him or his own.

-Expressing God-love in friendship is acting towards and loving your friends in the same manner God loves. It expresses what we've seen about God-love in nurturing, loving, caring, encouraging and growing the relationship you have with your friends in a way that allows you and them to be the most in life.

You may have a friend that is like a brother to you and that you love like a brother. When you have this very close relationship with a friend it takes on the dynamics of family with all the wonderful and difficult interactions that go with being in a family. So, it's the same God-love working with the same love principles, but your dynamics are different because of your level of intimacy. This type of very close friendship requires special care and thought, a cultivated awareness based in love.

-Christian love for one another: 1 Peter 3:8-9 "Finally, all of you be of one mind, having compassion for one another; love as brothers, be tender-hearted, be courteous; not returning evil for evil or reviling for reviling, but on the contrary blessing, knowing that you were called to this, that you may inherit a blessing." This is another expression of love in the bible and is most commonly used in the church to illustrate the kind of love we must have for fellow believers - not as ones who believe the same as we, but as ones joined in one bloodline through Christ. This shows how believers must love one another as if 'blood related' and gives some very clear examples and directives of what this brotherly love should translate to, in action.

God-love flows through us to every part of our life and every interaction. By the very nature of God-love, we express love through care. Galatians 6:10 "Therefore, as we have opportunity, let us do good to all, especially to those who are of the household of faith." How do we treat fellow believers? The key is in the word 'household', implying family unit or of the same family. We treat and care for the brothers and sisters in Christ as we care for our own household. This is the love that shows, in action, that what we have belongs to and is at the disposal of those in the household of faith who have need. It is beautifully illustrated in Acts 4:32-35 showing how they held all things in common for the benefit of the whole community of believers and for the furtherance of the Gospel.

Colossians 3:14 "But above all these things put on love, which is the bond of perfection." **Paul is teaching on the character of kingdom believers. Perfection is operating in the full grown manner that shows the new mind operating in full multi-dimensional knowledge. To do that effectively, we do it in love.**

By cultivating a life lived in God-love it becomes our default setting in all our actions, including to the stranger or anyone we encounter. This is one of the greatest opportunities to express God-love to those who do not know. Action is far greater than words, so think of little ways you can express God-love. When that overworked server in your favourite restaurant brings your order. You might say, 'We're about to pray over our food, is there anything we can pray for you?' I've had the most amazing responses in restaurants to this simple caring question. Follow it up with leaving that server a really nice tip and a smile when you leave. Or pay for the groceries of the person behind you in line, give them a big smile and wish them a wonderful day. These little things can make a huge difference in another person's life and God will use it in profound ways.

Let's talk about sex.

Sexual love is a gift of God, given for enjoyment and union between two who are one in a marriage covenant. Sexual longing and sexual desire are from God. The entire book of Song of Solomon expresses sexual longing and sexual desire, with each chapter deepening the realization of true love and culminating in the expression of complete, surrendered, and unselfish love - love that is God.

-It's part of marriage: 1 Corinthians 7:2-5 - Sexual pleasure is clearly meant for two people joined in marriage. Sexual union is part of the whole package of this love and is to be enjoyed regularly.

-Sex has a spiritual principle: 1 Corinthians 6:16-18 - When sex is used in casual relationships it can create a 'soul tie' that binds you to a person and can create an unwholesome mental and emotional binding to that person which can stop you from growing healthy relationships. This scripture shows there is a spiritual principle behind the physical act of sex: you are tied to the person you have sex with on a very deep level that cements your relationship in a way that makes you one. Genesis 2:24. This is why it's important in marriage because it actually 'makes one' on a spiritual level.

-Couples have freedom in their sexual practice. Hebrews 13:4 "Marriage is honourable among all, and the bed undefiled." This is a point of discussion. Find out what your partner likes and discuss what gives you most pleasure. Be open and frank and remember this is for both of you to enjoy.

Ephesians 5:28 & 33 "So husbands ought to love their own wives as their own bodies; he who loves his wife loves himself...and let the wife see that she respects her husband." Keeping in mind husbands are to be like Christ is to the church in their treatment of the wife and wives should respect husbands, neither should force the other to do things in sex they aren't comfortable with. Sex is there for both, a union to 'make one,' (Ephesians 5:31), so what gives you greater intimacy? Marriage is the ultimate union of two, being and living as one, where God-love can find full expression and become a power to grow and deepen your relationship with your partner. Take time to grow in this.

Everything is saturated in God-love, waiting to find full expression in your life. Let it. Allow God-love to change you and the way you love and relate to yourself, others and God. Allow it to be dynamic and creative in you and through you by learning to walk in its fullness. Grow in your thinking and understanding of God-love and carefully and thoughtfully find ways you can express love daily.

Having seen the power and scope of God-love, let's look at the juice that propels your life and how to harness it...

JUICE TO FUEL YOUR PASSION

Joy is the juice your life runs on

God and eternal heaven exude joy. It's present throughout heaven and is one of the reasons why joyful praise and simple gratitude is so powerful – it connects us to the source of our joy. Psalm 33:1 shows praise pleases God and is considered beautiful. God is joyful and delights in us and we see how His love and joy pour out towards us in Zephaniah 3:17 "The Lord your God in your midst, The mighty One will save, He will rejoice over you with gladness, He will quiet you with His love, He will rejoice over you with singing."

That's God in unrestrained joy over His creation 'quieting' us with His love. **He is in effect saying, 'Just have joy, live in joy, My love has done everything.'** And that is why living a life of gratitude releases so much abundance. It's also one of the reasons why real, intentioned and focused praise opens heaven and brings instant contact with the full presence of God and the power of heavenly praise.

Eternal heaven is a happy place, filled with joyful sounds. As God laid the foundation of creation joy filled eternal heaven. Job 38:7 "When the morning stars sang together, and all the sons of God shouted for joy." The angels delighted in the creation of God. They watched the power of God's words form and shape the worlds, create time and space, and from God-infused dust form human beings. **Creation was a noisy affair, with great and loud joy expressed by the angels.**

And the angels continue to have joyful interest and involvement in creation. Luke 15:10 "there is joy in the presence of the angels of God over one sinner who repents." **They see this as the return of creation to the intended state and delight when a believer accesses the kingdom and lives there.** Nothing has changed. Joy fills eternal heaven.

The joy continues because it's the default setting of heaven. Let's take a peek at what John saw on a day while he worshipped on the Isle of Patmos: A new song is sung in Revelation 5:8, when Jesus takes the scroll, and in Revelation 5:11-14 angels, living creatures, elders and thousands and thousands of others worship and declare God's goodness. **Heaven is filled with the happy sounds of joy and Jesus taught the power of joy.**

Full joy.

These are some of the final words of Jesus to prepare His disciples for His departure and for them to assume all He had operated in. John 15:11 "These things I have spoken to you, that My joy may remain in you, and that your joy may be full." In His final words, He's not teaching them to heal the sick or raise the dead, He's saying 'stay in My joy that roots and grounds you in the kingdom'. He combines this joy with reminding them He has appointed them to bear lasting fruit so that when His disciples ask, they will receive (verse 16) and reminds them to do it all in God-love. **Real and lasting joy works at its full power in God-love – love and joy** dovetail with the other Fruit to produce the environment for dynamic and powerful, balanced, fruitful living.

They had seen the power of joy operating in the life of Jesus. He used kingdom joy to get Him through the darkest time of His earthly existence. Hebrews 12:2 "...Who for the joy that was set before Him endured the cross, despising the shame, and has sat down at the right hand of the throne of God." **Because joy was His default setting, Jesus could face His ultimate sacrifice with the perspective of what is gained.** Joy will take you through the dark and hard places and motivate you to keep going to the end goal. David understood this. Psalm 23.

Jesus leaves His joy with us and seals it in a prayer to the Father. John 17:13 "...that they may have My joy fulfilled in themselves." Why is joy so important that it's included in one of the last prayers of Jesus on earth? It's the juice of your life and will grease your life – it's a propelling force that enables you to face anything in life happily. **We don't just live in this joy, we do something with it.**

We have a great deal of control whether we respond to or react to life and living. We also can develop happiness and joy and the emotional intelligence to navigate the hard places in life and turn them into learning and growing times. **Paul is a good example to follow in these times. He mastered the ability to think 'right' even in wrong situations.** Philippians 4:4 "Rejoice in the Lord always. I will say it again: Rejoice!." Paul is in prison uncertain if he'll be freed or executed yet his habit of thinking 'right' (Philippians 4:8) sustains him and allows him to empower others too. **He demonstrates firstly that bad events don't require us to feel awful and secondly that healthy thinking allows us to control our feelings.**

Deep joy.

This is an unchanging joy that remains and is evident in us. And like all Fruit of the Spirit, it produces. Jesus teaches about the faithful servant who took the talents given by his king and faithfully multiplied and grew what was entrusted to him until his master's return. **This is a powerful principle of living in joy: growing and increasing what God entrusted to you. Although this has spiritual aspects, Jesus purposely used a commercial setting to stress it's growing all areas of life, not just spiritually.** Why? God-love is dynamic and creates, increases, gives, enhances, because that is what it is designed to do. So everything you've been given has this design and when you operate in that design you see the result Matthew 25:23 "...Enter into the joy of your lord." **This is the deep joy of living so aligned with the dynamic power in God-love that all the joy of heaven flows through you.**

Psalm 16:11 "You show me the path of life; In your presence is fullness of joy; At Your right hand are pleasures forevermore."

Remember when we looked at you as a multi-dimensional being? **Heaven is all around the time tunnel we live in and because of your very nature, you need to connect inter-dimensionally to feed your inter-dimensionality.** What does this mean? To nourish your body you eat, sleep, hydrate, exercise and purposely find ways to actively enhance your life. Nourishing your mind, you build healthy thought patterns, you study, improve your mind, grow emotional intelligence, operate in balanced emotions and grow the Fruit, interact and relate and do all the other things that help your mind to grow and function at its full potential. Nourishing your spirit happens in your time with God, in growing in the Spirit and your knowledge of the kingdom and learning how to live and move in the kingdom. It's applying the things we've covered in this book that enable you to live a dynamic, whole and happy life. You live from the limitless perspective of your multi-dimensionality. It's a joyful place to be.

Receiving in joy.

John 16:24 "Until now you have asked nothing in My name, Ask, and you will receive that your joy may be full." Jesus gave us access to the kingdom and we're joint-heirs with Him. So it's like you going to the abundant storehouse of heaven to get something you really, really want and saying, 'My big brother said I can ask for this,' and receiving it. **Joy creates an expectant heart because the very foundation of joy is God-love, so you know the very best, the very most abundant is yours.**

If you're at a point in your life where your intentions have not materialised and you are still moving to the fulfilment of your goal, take lots and lots of time in joy. **Practise gratitude as a way of life by taking a moment of time, many times during the day to just stop, focus, be in the moment and find something to thank God for.** Also, make sure you have written down your goals and intentions to make them real and don't forget to date what you write down. Most importantly, go over your list from time to time so you can spend time appreciating what you have received on the list. Like Jesus, use joy for what is ahead, your final goal, to keep you going.

My partner and I keep a box called 'special events' with little cards filled with the amazing things God has done in our lives, the prayers He answered and the miracles we've seen. And in dark and hard times, I'd take out that little box, reach into it and randomly pick one of the hundreds of cards in there. It would lift my spirit and I'd usually end up in praise or gratitude. **Find little life hacks you can incorporate into your life to keep you in joy.**

Grow through joy.

Psalm 119:162 "I rejoice at Your word, as one who finds great treasure." By understanding what we have in God fully, joy is released. It's utterly mind boggling in abundance and extent. Spend time with Him and in the Word and take time to really look at your life and what you have in treasure as a result of your relationship and knowledge. You know this. **Take some time and use the same passion and intention and attention given to achieving your goals in discovering more about God and the kingdom. It'll feed your joy, increase your ability to live a dynamic life and open knowledge to you and produce growth in you...**

Juiced and Ready!

Intentional joyful living.

If we are thoughtful in seeking opportunities to express the manifested Fruit of joy, it follows that more joy will be expressed in more areas of our lives. It is the juice that fuels our lives, even in the midst of hardship and is, at times of barrenness or frustration, the only thing that will propel us to the mountaintop. Happiness requires circumstances to flourish, whereas joy bubbles up regardless of what is going on about us. **Cultivating joy is simply choosing to release and yield to the joy of the Lord, having confidence in Him. We let God be God.** It requires us taking our eyes off the world, the circumstances and the people and holding onto our destiny with our eyes fixed on Jesus.

Philippians 4: 4-5 "Rejoice in the Lord always. Again, I will say, rejoice! Let your gentleness be known to all men. The Lord is at hand." Why is this so very important? What is the reason for making joy one of the manifestations of the Fruit of the Holy Spirit? We find when we walk in this joy focused on the Lord, His strength is released in and through us. **It's tangibly noticeable and that makes it contagious, uplifting because it silently testifies that you have something wonderful in your life.** It radiates out from you, you light up a room, people smile when they see you because they pick up that the whole field that surrounds you is joy. It's attractive and attracting.

Nehemiah 8:10b "…Do not sorrow, for the joy of the Lord is your strength." Cultivating this must become our prime concern. It does not mean we will never have sorrow. It's being rooted in joy, even in the midst of sorrow. **Finding the right things to fill our life with, the right love to fill our heart with and the right thoughts to fill our mind with goes a long way to living a life of rejoicing.** This starts with the right mindset.

This is thoughtful joyfulness in action.

Our perspective determines our reality. So, where we put our focus and our emphasis will determine what we believe of the world, God's power and our victory or defeat in life. Philippians 4:8 TLB "Finally, brethren, whatever things are true, whatever things are noble, whatever things are just, whatever things are pure, whatever things are lovely, whatever things are of good report, if there is any virtue and if there is anything praiseworthy - meditate on these things." **God remains constant and the manifestation of the Fruit of the Holy Spirit is ever present - we are the only variable.**

Philippians 1:12-14 "But I want you to know, brethren,

that the things that happened to me have actually turned out for the furtherance of the gospel, so that it has become evident to the whole palace guard, and to all the rest, that my chains are in Christ; and that most of the brethren in the Lord, having become confident in my chains, are much more bold to speak the word without fear." What should have been a setback was viewed by Paul as progress of the Gospel. Victims ask: "Why me?" As Fruit bearers we ask: "What is the furtherance for the Gospel and my personal growth in this?" Even when you're afraid in the circumstances or you're not sure of the outcome, follow Paul and stay in joy. It's not in circumstances but in what we believe those circumstances determine in the form of action and change in us and obedience in what God uses the circumstance for. This is a growth mindset that is one of the best psychological tools to use in conjunction with the Fruit to grow your life in difficult times.

Joy and submission.

Paul uses Christ as the perfect example in Philippians 2:5-8. **Everything that was involved in Jesus becoming human began with an attitude of submission, a willingness to cooperate with God's plan for salvation.** He endured the shame of the cross for the joy that obedience brought. Because Jesus was willing, we see what ultimately happened. **We are the living and eternally lasting proof that the joy set before Jesus was real and brought lasting results. When joy operates in a life, powerful things happen.**

Philippians 2:9-11 "Therefore also God highly exalted Him, and bestowed on Him the name which is above every name, that at the name of Jesus every knee should bow, of those who are in heaven, and on earth, and under the earth, and that every tongue should confess that Jesus Christ is

Lord, to the glory of God the Father." **Just like Jesus, hold onto your end goal when you're moving through something by joyfully remembering what you're heading to. And let the power of joy work in your life when you receive your prize. In every circumstance and every situation, let joy flow.**

Active Joyfulness

1 Thessalonians 1:6 "And you became followers of us and of the Lord, having received the word in much affliction, with joy of the Holy Spirit." Really look at this Scripture. They received the word from a persecuted Paul, in persecution themselves. What kept them on course? The joy of the Holy Spirit! As Comforter, He uses joy to turn the focus of pain, persecution, or loss into a new dimension of union with God. **It's also a time where tremendous personal growth takes place if we guard our hearts against anger or bitterness and remain in joy.** Active joyfulness enables us to stay the course.

Philemon 7 "For we have great joy and consolation in your love, because the hearts of the saints have been refreshed by you, brother." The word for 'joy' here means 'gracious manner to act.' **Active joyfulness is gracious in dealing with others, knows how to acknowledge and thank those around them and seeks to be a transforming force through their joy.** Good manners are a small way to make way for this facet of joy to manifest. By acting lovingly, we allow the contagion of joy to flow through to draw others to want what we have.

Psalm 35:27a "Let them shout for joy and be glad, who favour my righteous cause…" Real joy is dynamic, genuine, and evident! Active joyfulness uses the manifestation of joy as a form of proclamation and praise. There is great power in this facet of joy. Psalm 132:9 "Let Your priests be clothed with righteousness and let Your saints shout for joy." This is the triumphant joy expressed in singing or shouting that brings about deliverance and victory. **We saw the same facet of joy expressed in the Old Testament when Joshua led the people in a great shout that flattened the walls of Jericho. When we operate in the Fruit and live in joy, we release its power.** This abandon in joy creates an amazing conduit for God to work through and extraordinary things happen, just like the Jericho incident above.

And God will use it in the most amazing and miraculous ways. We have many, many examples of joy changing things in our lives but here is one small everyday example. It's from a time when we were missionaries and experiencing a period of financial challenge. Let's put this miracle into context for you, on this day, we had no money, the cupboards were almost bare and we were expecting dinner guests. There I am, standing in the kitchen looking at the little I have - a half cup of mince and half a can of baked beans. What am I to do? I'm going to make chilli.

And then God gives me an instruction:

"Say, 'Praise the Lord' and whilst you keep doing so, stir the mince in the pot clockwise as you cook it." That's it. We were used to God giving instructions that were unusual, to say the least. It had become quite the norm. So, I followed this instruction, exactly as told. I put the handful of mince at the bottom of a large pot and started cooking. "Praise the Lord." I stir clockwise. "Praise the Lord... praise the Lord." I keep on stirring and keep on saying the words. In front of my eyes, that small amount of mince at the bottom of the pot began growing and growing. Once it browned, I added the beans and kept stirring. There's an elevated excitement in my tone. "Praise the Lord... praise the Lord, praise the Lord." The beans multiply and the mixture keeps rising in the pot until it fills the pot to the top. All that was left to do was add spices. Our guests arrived and we enjoyed a delicious, chilli dinner joyfully. After everyone had eaten, there was a generous amount left.

Joyful abandon in giving and receiving.

Joy in giving is another way the Fruit empowers a very ordinary act (generosity) with knock-on effects. 2 Corinthians 9:7 "So let each one give as he purposes in his heart, not grudgingly or out of necessity; for God loves a cheerful giver." Cheerful means a propitious or merry, prompt, and willing giver. **If we attain joy in all our giving, we release the 'juice of joy' to work in the area of cheerful giving. This dynamic force infuses the gift of generosity with the Spirit and amazing things happen.** It works with money or loving relationships or any other area where the principle of sowing and reaping works.

Joy in receiving is just as important and has the same power working through it, just in reverse. James 1:17 "Every good gift and every perfect gift is from above, and comes down from the Father of lights, with whom there is no variation or shadow of turning." God gives very great gifts and we must receive without reservation every gift given. **Doubting salvation, God's love or the Gifts and Fruit of the Holy Spirit are all ways of not being a joyful receiver.**

God also moves others to bless us. Philippians 4:17 "Not that I seek the gift but I seek the fruit that abounds to your account." Receiving joyfully a gift given is as important as being a cheerful giver. In doing this, we open the way for the giver to receive the blessing of being a good giver and so complete the cycle of blessing tied to giving and receiving. **In receiving joyfully with the same heart as our giving, we open a door of blessing to those who gave by releasing the 'juice of joy' in the situation so the Spirit can flow**

both ways. See how joy is constantly greasing the tracks of your life in hundreds of ways?

Harmony promotes joy.

Philippians 2:1-2 "Therefore if there is any consolation in Christ, if any comfort of love, if any fellowship of the Spirit, if any affection and mercy, fulfil my joy by being like-minded, having the same love, being of one accord, of one mind." This is having a like-minded spirit with one another, by living life in unity with a genuine, Spirit-filled unselfishness that breeds strength and spreads joy. We looked at the way God-love expresses in church, as we treat fellow believers as family in our love and care. Like-mindedness means we seek the same goals and hold the same vision. There's tremendous strength in this for the church and each individual involved. You can fall back on the one-mindedness of your body of believers for the times you experience doubt about God or His Word.

We will also have times when we need to 'press forward' in joy. Practising gratitude as a daily routine is a great way to make you aware of all the good in your life even in the midst of hardship. **By taking 5 minutes and focusing on 5 things you are grateful for with a heart focused on the benefits and blessing in those 5 things will change your day. According to the latest scientific research, it will lift your mood, make you more aware, more compassionate and bring good change to your physical brain. That's the power of gratitude.**

Remember, the Fruit of the Spirit works Spirit to mind, so your mental abilities are involved in enlarging it in your life. By assessing our lives carefully to see where we need harmony and balance or where we lack joy, we can then use psychological cognitive tools and prayer to bring change where needed.

Enhance your joy.

Psalm 16:11 "You will show me the path of life; in Your presence is fullness of joy; at Your right hand are pleasures forevermore." **Joy floods eternal heaven, so if you'd like to get closer to God, enhance joy in your life.** How do we do that? Joy is found in an abiding and yielded life. **The best way to reach back to a place of joy is to reach up to the throne of God.** Remember, God loves you as much as He loves Jesus John 17:10 and pursues you passionately. He wants His joy to flow through you and enrich and enlarge your life. 1 John 1:3-4 "that which we have seen and heard we declare to you, that you also may have fellowship with us; and truly our fellowship is with the Father and with His Son Jesus Christ. And these things we write to you that your joy may be full."

John 15 shows us that in the abiding and fruit bearing life we find the manifested Fruit of the Spirit flowing in our lives. Romans 14:17 "for the kingdom of God is not food and drink, but righteousness and peace and joy in the Holy Spirit." Translating the meaning of joy, we find that it manifests as 'cheerfulness, a calm delight or exceeding gladness'. That calm, deep joy that bubbles up to bring joy to your life and the lives of all you encounter.

That's the Spirit investment - joy. We take that investment and allow it to flow out as cheerfulness that shows as animated, and a life with the quality of being 'in good spirits', very literally! Acts 13:52 " And the disciples were filled with joy and the Holy Spirit." **What a happy way to be a conduit of power and joy to others!** You see this is yours now, so, if you feel joy is lacking in your life, ask, receive and enjoy. Psalm 51:12 "Restore to me the joy of Your salvation, and uphold me with Your generous Spirit." The beauty of God's mercy in the manifestation of the Fruit of the Spirit is that we can ask to have our joy restored when we have lost it and have the immediate assurance bubbling up in us that our joy is back.

A great way to do this is just by counting your blessings right now. Take a few minutes and look at your life and all you have as a believer. Take some of the scriptures we've looked at in this section and read them aloud so you can hear your own voice (this brings belief and acts as a declaration). Then, end off with a few moments of singing to God (have fun by making up a song or sing one of your favourites). Now, before you re-join the other parts of your life, lift your chin, square your shoulders, smile (you're signalling to your brain that you're happy and it will release feel-good endorphins to make it happen).

Maximizing the deposit of Joy. Some reasons to meditate on that will help joy flow.

-Rejoice in God's forever love for you: Romans 8:38-39 "For I am persuaded that neither death nor life, nor angels, nor principalities, nor powers, nor things present, nor things to come, nor height, nor depth, nor any other created thing, shall be able to separate us from the love of God which is in Christ Jesus our Lord." When we rejoice in the message of John 3:16, we know that the saving grace of God is the beginning of His love that extends into the eternal future with Him.

-Rejoice in eternal redemption that is ours: Romans 5:8 & 21 "But God demonstrates His own love towards us, in that while we were still sinners, Christ died for us. ... so that as sin reigned in death, even so grace might reign through righteousness to eternal life through Jesus Christ our Lord." We rejoice that we have life eternally and life abundantly right now as kingdom dwellers and that we will continue forever if we remain in Christ and yielded to Him. We are part of His kingdom with all the benefits and blessings that entails.

-Rejoice in knowing your name is written in the Book of Life: Luke 10:20 "Nevertheless do not rejoice in this that the spirits are subject to you, but rather rejoice because your names are written in heaven." Our power is not cause for rejoicing but rather the fact that we are registered kingdom dwellers. This scripture also shows God loves us so much that at birth He places our names in the Book of Life and leaves it there until death, so that we may have the opportunity to avail ourselves of the saving grace of Jesus. What love! He only finally relinquishes His passionate pursuit of us at death if we have chosen not to love Him in return. Revelation 3:5.

-Rejoice, God created us with a destiny and unique purpose: Ephesians 2:10 "For we are His workmanship, created in Christ Jesus for good works, which God prepared beforehand that we should walk in them." Our destiny is set out by God, but our choice is revealed in our attitude toward God, others, and life. The amazing fact about calling is that it was 'prepared beforehand'. That means before we were born there was prepared a very specific calling and unique destiny to fulfil that only finds completion in Christ.

-Rejoice you are uniquely made and loved. 2 Timothy 1:9 "who has saved us and called us with a holy calling, not according to our works, but according to His own purpose and grace which was given to us in Christ Jesus before time began." God knew and purposely made each of us in a specific way for a definite reason. No one person is an accident. Each has a unique mix of gifts, callings and talents that make up their spiritual DNA and determines who they are in the scheme of things. Whether we believe it or not, we are important and have a part to play in the great unfolding drama of life and eternity.

-Rejoice because His Power and Presence lives in you: 1 John 4:4 "You are of God, little children, and have overcome them, because He who is in you is greater than he who is in the world." We have all the power and authority that was available to Jesus resident in us. We have the glory of God contained in our bodies and the very Spirit of God chooses to dwell in us, love us and empower us for life with full access to everything in God's kingdom.

-Rejoice you have Spirit life. Romans 8:11 "But if the Spirit of Him who raised Jesus from the dead dwells in you, He who raised Christ from the dead will also give life to your mortal bodies through His Spirit who dwells in you." The Spirit who raised Jesus with all His abilities and power lives in us! If all of the enemy's minions and death itself could not hold sway against the Spirit of God raising Jesus, what could overcome you with Him inside you?

-Rejoice you have light and bear light. 2 Corinthians 4: 6 "For it is the God who commanded light to shine out of darkness who has shone in our hearts to give the light of the knowledge of the glory of God in the face of Jesus Christ." The knowledge and renewal of our understanding of Christ releases the light of knowledge of God's glory. There is only one place to find the fullness of that - in the face of Jesus. In other words, in an up close and personal relationship that unfolds daily. As light bearer, renew yourself daily with face time with God.

-Rejoice, you have what you need: 1 Corinthians 15:57-58 "But thanks be to God, who gives us the victory through our Lord Jesus Christ. Therefore, my beloved brethren, be steadfast, immovable, always abounding in the work of the Lord, knowing that your labour is not in vain in the Lord." As long as we live and move and have our existence in Jesus, we are assured of victory here on earth and in eternity to come. We have overcome death in Christ, and we live in eternal life in the kingdom right here and now.

-Rejoice you have the victory. 1 John 5:4-5 "For whatever is born of God overcomes the world. And this is the victory that has overcome the world - our faith. Who is he who overcomes the world, but he who believes that Jesus is the Son of God?" We know the outcome and understand that the final victory is complete in Calvary. At the cross, Jesus once and for always sealed the victory, it is merely manifesting in time and space. Our life in Him is sure if we stay in Him.

-Rejoice, we are, and have, the Body of Christ: 1 Thessalonians 1:6 "And you became followers of us and of the Lord, having received the word in much affliction, with joy of the Holy Spirit." We flesh out Jesus to a dying world and show His face of love to all who are caught in wrong thinking and doing and wandering in the dark.

-Rejoice in the collective joy of the Body of Christ. 2 Timothy 1:4 "greatly desiring to see you, being mindful of your tears, that I may be filled with joy." The power of the unity and transforming relationships we share with others in the Body brings great joy in the same way the health of our physical parts brings health to our whole physical body. But more than that, we are part of His Body and His kingdom with all other believers of all time. What power in the collective prayers and actions over 2000 years! The whole Body, flowing in the power and prayer of all its individual members, constantly strengthening and being strengthened.

The whole of heaven is filled with joy and joy is a power source both above and below. Your life runs on the juice of joy and you have full access to its full enabling power through the Fruit of the Spirit. Romans 5:2 "through whom also we have access by faith into this grace in which we stand, and rejoice in the hope of the glory of God."

Understanding God-love and flowing in joy we release one of our greatest weapons and sweetest gifts…

AT ONE AGAIN

Peace gives wholeness in our mental realm to bring completion and sets us at one again.

Let's look at what that means. "'Peace to you! As the Father has sent Me, I also send you!' And when He had said this, He breathed on them, and said to them 'Receive the Holy Spirit.'" John 20:21. **The resurrected Jesus starts His first greeting after His resurrection with "peace to you". Jesus is making a profound point and sets the tone of where He is about to take the disciples mentally.** This handful of followers are about to go out as Jesus' representatives, alone. **John 20:21 is both a blessing and an empowering.** Jesus is empowering them ahead of receiving the Spirit without measure and the Fruit that will enable them to function in wholeness in their mission. What they saw Him do, they must now copy.

Jesus gave His peace to us.

This flow in the Fruit was evident in all the areas of Jesus' life. And it is clear that He used His cognitive abilities to show how we should respond as humans. **When He confronted the enemy, He didn't do so with His** emotions or in fear. **Knowing that the enemy was a liar, He simply refused to be influenced by any voice other than God's and remained grounded in peace. His peace overwhelmed the enemy; His authority then shattered the lie, which sent demons fleeing.** Jesus lived as a Spirit-empowered man to give us an example of how to centre our lives in peace and experience the resultant wholeness.

The word for 'peace' needs closer examination to understand what is offered in this manifestation of the Fruit. **As love is the centre of our actions and life walk, peace is the core of our wholeness in God.** The word used for 'peace' translates as 'one, quietness, rest, set at one again'. **It is much more than a restful or quiet place, it's a point of total restoration.** Set at one again' implies a restoration back to wholeness and completeness where everything is complete. Think of a situation where you heaved a sigh of completion at the end of some great task, and that gives a very poor glimpse of what this peace feels like.

Colossians 1:19-20: "For it pleased the Father that in Him all the fullness should dwell, and by Him to reconcile all things to Himself, by Him, whether things on earth or things in heaven, having made peace through the blood of His cross." He enabled us to be 'at one' again with God and He upholds that peace eternally. Jesus is the 'harmonizer' that brings the reality of that peace to a fallen and marred creation. **He 'set at one again' through His peace so we could enjoy this kingdom state of being here on earth. He used His blood offered in peace to release our reconciliation!**

Jesus is the Prince of peace (Isaiah 9:6) and we who are in Him have the right to live in the fullness of His peace that has made us whole. **As the Prince of peace, He rules over the peace He purchased.** John 14:27 "Peace I leave with you, My peace I give to you; not as the world gives do I give to you. Let not your heart be troubled, neither let it be afraid." **In effect, this is not an earthly peace, it's the peace that passes all understanding and contains in it the power to overcome anything.** Jesus had operated as a Spirit-empowered man while on earth to release the full power and potential of kingdom peace on us, "for He is our peace" Ephesians 2:14.

Let's look at other examples where Jesus lived and functioned in the manifestation of the Fruit.

Jesus practised peace.

Every situation in His life is an object lesson on how He lived and manifested peace. **You see, peace is not just feeling and living 'at-one', it extends to and influences all your living and life.** Let's look into Jesus in the midst of a storm. Although we know in this account that Jesus must have been very tired, we know that He slept through the storm, not because of His fatigue but because He was at total peace. Mark 4:37-40 "And a great windstorm arose, and the waves beat into the boat, so that it was already filling. But He was in the stern, asleep on a pillow. And they awoke Him and said to Him, 'Teacher, do You not care that we are perishing?' Then He arose and rebuked the wind, and said to the sea, 'Peace, be still!' And the wind ceased and there was a great calm. But He said to them, 'Why are you so fearful? How is it that you have no faith?'"

He deals with their focus not their situation. The disciples saw the waves and the wind and the water filling the boat (that was the real situation) and concluded that they were perishing (an unproven conclusion). **Jesus was no doubt aware of the storm but because He had a different conclusion based in peace, He sleeps on.** He remains calm when they wake Him and addresses the very thing that caused so much fear and unbelief and speaks these very specific words: "Peace, be still."

Jesus' peace overwhelmed the waves and the wind - when He then spoke in authority, nature not only obeyed, but a great calm also descended. He never denied the reality of the wind, the waves, or the water in the boat, He trusted God and relied on the Spirit's Fruit to guide His actions. **In the centre of the wholeness that the manifestation of the Fruit of peace brings, He extends that peace beyond the boat to all nature. He speaks in total authority of the empowering Spirit and nature obeys.** This is the power of the peace found in the Fruit of Spirit. And it's available to you.

Peace works.

At one time, we lived in an area of the United States known for its tornadoes and hurricanes. When the storms came, I would go to my quiet place, bring myself to the present, listen to God and juice up, and then just do what He says about the storm. Many times it simply took a 'Peace, be still,' at other times I'd be told to pray in specific ways or do a specific thing. The amazing thing is, it worked. The storm would dissipate, or lessen or turn over the sea. And when it did make landfall where we were, we never suffered damage.

Once, with a tornado barrelling down on our home, we prayed and heard a 'Ka-dunk' on the roof. Looking up I saw an angel on our roof, sent for our protection. We lived on a huge piece of land that was densely forested, with tall pine trees on the property. A tornado around our home would have seriously damaged it and the huge trees would have flattened our house and endangered our lives. We sat in peace inside our house – we heard the noise of the tornado, then the absolute stillness in the midst of it and then...nothing. It was over. We went outside in the morning. Trees close to our home were snapped and splintered but what should have landed on our roof was simply not there. Surrounding the house everything in the bubble of peace maintained by that angel had remained exactly the same. Peace works in many ways.

This is a good place to stress again that the Fruit of the Spirit must work with the wisdom of God. Don't copy what others are doing in their flow of the Fruit, find out how God chooses to flow through you. Peace and the fullness of that peace is available to us to use and to influence every area of our lives. And it all started with Jesus showing us what peace is, how to live in it and how to use it in all the places of our life. Romans 8:6-7 "For to be carnally minded is death, but to be spiritually minded is life and peace. Because the carnal mind is enmity against God; for it is not subject to the law of God, nor indeed can be." **Jesus not only came and preached peace, but He is also the doorway for that peace that is found only through the Holy Spirit.**

At One Living

All kingdom dwellers have access to this peace because it's living and being 'at one' with God. It's harmonious, plugged in living in the kingdom.

Romans 10:15 "And how shall they preach unless they are sent? As it is written: 'How beautiful are the feet of those who preach the gospel of peace, who bring glad tidings of good things.'" **The very first place peace sets us at one again is with God. We are reconciled to Him and we then become the carriers of this manifestation of the Holy Spirit to passionately pursue and set others at one**

again with God.

You have this peace regardless of circumstances, good or bad, to operate in, and peace is equally present in both. So, no matter what is happening in your life or where you need to bring 'at one-ment' to, you have this power available to you. **It brings a wholeness to the mental realm to aid us to reach beyond everything in a 'set at one again' state and operate from that vantage regardless of our own emotional defects.** When this manifestation is evident, our inner world no longer wars against ourselves, against God and against those we love.

Peace and joy are linked in some scriptures to show the wholeness of peace uses the fuel of joy to move us forward.

Romans 15:13 "Now may the God of hope fill you with all joy and peace in believing, that you may abound in hope by the power of the Holy Spirit." We are 'set at one again' and with the 'juice of joy' have the ability to have the biblical hope that has expectation of achieving its goal within a time frame. **So, it progresses: Love is the fountainhead of everything. Joy fuels our passion and peace gives wholeness in our mental realm to bring completion.**

If the enemy can steal your joy, he can undermine your peace. Why? Joy is the juice we run on. Romans 14:17 "for the kingdom of God is not food and drink, but righteousness and peace and joy in the Holy Spirit." **The righteousness of God in Christ Jesus is the position we hold as we relate and transform in the 'set at one again' state by using the juice of joy to fuel our life and our walk.**

Proverbs 14:30a "A sound heart is life to the body." So many believers walk about never allowing the fullness of this manifestation of the Fruit to fuel their life due to the bad teaching they have received. Many quote Matthew 10:34 that clearly states that Jesus did not come to bring peace to the earth but a sword. However, looking at the verses that follow we see that this refers to the great offense the gospel brings that often even divides families. The sword is the Word and the Word weighs and divides. Hebrews 4:12 "For the word of God is living and powerful, and sharper than any two-edged sword, piercing even to the division of soul and spirit, and of joints and marrow, and is a discerner of the thoughts and intents of the heart." **Peace empowers whole living and is a force for change.**

Expanding peace.

James 3:18 "Now the fruit of righteousness is sown in peace by those who make peace."

I shared the story of my dealings with hurricanes and tornadoes because I want to show that peace, and indeed any manifestation of the Fruit, is a force to be used in every area of our lives. **Jesus lived peace, related in peace and used peace this way. He taught His disciples to do the same.**

With the disciples about to be sent out by Jesus, He tells them in Matthew 10:12-13 "And when you go into a household, greet it. If the household is worthy, let your peace come upon it. But if it is not worthy, let your peace return to you." Jesus is preparing to send out His disciples and is showing what they need and how they should act. Peace here is the Fruit which is 'prosperity, quietness and at-one ment.' **Wherever you go, you as a Fruit-filled kingdom believer carry with you the power to bring real, tangible peace.** Notice 'let your peace come upon it,' **it's a tangible force of peace you are imparting on the household and you do it through purposely intentioning it.** You, as peace-carrier have control over this blessing and if that household cannot receive it, you take that back.

By teaching the disciples that this peace is a gift that can be imparted to a house that offered hospitality, He's showing them they can give their hosts something precious in return for their generosity. And it's not limited to households. We've given the gift of peace to regions and over whole countries and seen amazing change as a result. In flowing in peace like this, just remember Fruit is backed by all the power of the Spirit, so there is enough peace power to cover the whole world. **Your part is to be the conduit and to seek out places where you can offer peace.** Why not start right now? **Take a few minutes to pray and carefully think where your community or region is in conflict or where peace is needed.** Now, with the help of the Spirit and through careful thought, create a short blessing you will offer over the place in question. You may only need to do it once or you may speak it over the region for a while until the Fruit manifests. **Either way, you are using the principle Jesus taught of using peace as a blessing and an anointing.**

Recharging in peace.

By living through the grounded state of peace, we are able to approach each situation in the moment that it's occurring with a clear mind. Jesus achieved this by following some life habits like spending time with God in alone time, no matter how busy He was. It gave Him time to recharge, renew, relate and find the will of the Father. Sitting in quiet time with God, mentally present in that moment, He could plug in and just be. This state of being quiet and taking time to talk to God, listen and think about things brings profound and lasting results. **By being at peace and present in what is happening in the moment, your focus, attention and intention line up in 'at one-ness.'** You connect to eternal heaven and the creative voice of God, you release the power of the Fruit, the power of your mind, and your body and mind's ability to create and then do. **We see the result of**

Jesus' life habits and we continue to reap the benefits because He lived like this.

Freedom and wholeness.

Isaiah 26:3 "You will keep him in perfect peace, whose mind is stayed on You, Because He trusts in You." **This is the word 'shalom, peace,' which means 'health, prosperity and peace - wholly safe and well'. These are the marks of a kingdom person walking in the perfect peace of God given in the manifestation of the Fruit of the Holy Spirit.** This peace doesn't remove the hurt or harm of the world but brings into play the wholeness of God to meet every situation and circumstance head on in 'safeness and wellness' in God. It makes for calm, whole and wide-awake living.

Ephesians 2:17-18 "And He came and preached peace to you who were afar off and to those who were near. For through Him we both have access by one Spirit to the Father." Jesus preached and then demonstrated through the Spirit the truth of what He said. Do you notice Paul speaks of access to God in the same verse? **This peace is a grounded, clear-headed way of living where we don't allow anything contrary to what we know of God to influence us.** We operate in faith and trust and gain access to God because we apply Hebrews 11:16 "...for he that comes to God must believe that He is, and that He is a rewarder of those who diligently seek Him."

Peace as a Weapon.

In the battles of life, the Spirit's peace is actually a weapon. Living creates many situations that could rob you of your peace. Cash flow concerns, deadlines, relationships and all those things that form part of your daily living create stress on you. By following Jesus' example and remaining fully rooted in the moment and yielding to the Fruit you won't be moved from the centrality of your passion or God's love.

This great empowerment by the Spirit ensures we don't fear because God is with us. Born of our relationship with God, confidence in the God of peace releases the power of peace and declares that we don't accept the lies of the enemy or anything contrary to that peace. **Our ultimate reality - God ever constant, ever present. This is a perception we cultivate, a mindset that governs our thinking.** It is as you reach this point that you can declare in authority in the name of Jesus: "Peace, be still!" You have peace, Jesus gave it to you expecting you to use it. Matthew10:13.

Victory in peace.

By simply refusing to be influenced by any voice other than God's, the peace of the Spirit in you will overwhelm the enemy and any circumstance in life. All Christ's authority, working through you, will shatter the enemy's lie or life's circumstance, sending the enemy fleeing,

And when you have to face a circumstance that will not change, you face it, just like Jesus did, in facing the cross. You go through it in peace with the expectation of what will be achieved through it.

Here are His words to us to assure us it's a done deal: John 14:27 "Peace I leave with you; My peace I give to you; not as the world gives do I give to you. Let not your heart be troubled, neither let it be afraid." The price paid by Jesus for our peace motivates us to live in His peace. Isaiah 53:5b. It's given by Jesus, upheld by the Spirit and constantly at work in all areas of your life, if you let it.

The perspective of peace brings growth.

The battles you face will soon become a meal for you, an experience that will nourish and build you up spiritually and expand and grow you mentally, if you face it in the power of the Fruit. Looking at Psalm 23:5 David says, "You prepare a table for me in the presence of my enemies." **So, while your enemies look on, you sit down to enjoy a banquet prepared by the Lord Himself!** You're not removed from the situation, you're accessing God's abundance in the midst of your enemies. This is the extraordinary truth that results from not being influenced by emotions or fear but by being centred in the Spirit. **Treat what you are experiencing as a passing thing, a place where you will be abundantly nourished and enriched.** Ask God how you can grow in emotional intelligence through it and reach into the Spirit and anchor to the peace that is yours.

Grounded in Peace.

Only God's peace will quell our fleshly reactions in the everyday troubles of life. The source of the Spirit's peace is God Himself. **And when we purposely co-operate with the Fruit of peace through the use and control of our mind, we have victory. If fear has been knocking at your door, begin to face that fear with God's peace.** Romans 15:13 "Now the God of hope fill you with all joy and peace in believing, that you may abound in hope, through the power of the Holy Spirit." Look at that scripture again. Our peace is in our believing.

Here's a great exercise to keep you grounded in the peace of God.

When you find yourself moving from the centre of peace because of circumstances, **stop, breathe, bring yourself to this moment and follow this formula:**

I - Identify circumstances. What is <u>real</u>? What should your response be to that? (Reread the section on Jesus in the boat).

D - Detach yourself from jumping to a conclusion that is fear or circumstance based. Now look at the situation as it is now. Don't attach past 'stories' of similar circumstances to what is happening now. Pray and listen. Jesus saw the same waves and wind but His perspective was one of peace, so His conclusion was different.

D - Decide what Jesus would do and what the Holy Spirit has told you to do - which is always bible based.

A - Act in accordance with this under the flow of the Spirit and the Fruit. The best way out of fear is through considered action.

A uniting power.

God's peace is the common thread that unites the Body of Christ into a harmonious whole. **It 'sets at one again' the human race which was divided through wrong thinking and wrongdoing and opens the way for us to approach the Father in the wholeness His peace brings.** It also leads and guides in the way we must operate within this peace in the midst of the chaos of the world.

Philippians 4:6-7 "Be anxious for nothing, but in everything by prayer and supplication, with thanksgiving, let your requests be made known to God; and the peace of God, which surpasses all understanding, will guard your hearts and minds through Christ Jesus." **This peace does not just give us wholeness it also has the power to keep us God centred and calm in the midst of difficult situations.** And it hedges our minds and hearts to keep them from reverting to the patterns of wrong thinking and feeling. Thus, we can respond to all things with the mind of Christ.

Peace sets us at one with God, each other, and the world about us. It brings wholeness that enables us to flow in kingdom living in the power of God and our relationships.

WHOLESOME RELATIONSHIPS

**Longsuffering is mercy driven patience that teaches us
how to relate in love in dealing with people.**

We are inclined to lump biblical patience under one meaning.
By doing so, we are not getting the depth of the
manifestation of the Fruit of longsuffering. This is a
distinctive form of patience from the Greek word
'makrothumia' meaning 'to be longsuffering, forbearance,
self-restraint before proceeding to action'. It's 'the quality of a
person who is able to avenge themself yet refrains from doing
so.' **Very clearly, mercy drives this patience and this form
of patience obviously relates to people.**

That longsuffering is included in the Fruit clearly shows
God's heart. God is relational because He is love and He
deals with our dysfunctions in longsuffering. When our
behaviour is 'off' because of our skewed thinking, He delays
taking action and He's got a way to get us back on track.
Romans 2:4 "Or do you despise the riches of His goodness,
forbearance, and longsuffering, not knowing that the
goodness of God leads you to repentance?" God sets the
perfect example of longsuffering in how He deals with us and
the result of this leads to repentance. **When we exercise**

longsuffering, we offer an opportunity to someone through our mercy driven patience to be transformed. We can act and think like God by following His example.

Shrewd patience.

Walking in mercy driven patience is not about absence of discipline in church, home or self. The bible clearly lays out the discipline for the church and the home in circumstances where our wrong thinking impinges and brings harm. **We operate in longsuffering because of what we've been given by God.** Colossians 1:11-12 "Strengthened with all might, according to His glorious power, unto all patience and longsuffering with joyfulness… who has made us to be partakers of the inheritance of the saints in light." **It's part of our inheritance and is rooted in God's power, not our ability.** We use our mental abilities and kingdom knowledge to allow that power to flow through us.

Patience is not void of discernment and good, old-fashioned common sense. The mercy that inspires biblical patience contains an ingredient that overrides the temptation to judge or weigh another. Instead, just as Christ showed, we seek to restore and forgive the one in error. But we operate in this with emotional intelligence and under the direction of the Spirit. **In each situation in dealing with people, different dynamics are at play so we want to flow in longsuffering in an intelligent manner.** We need to consider what psychological and situational factors are at work and what is the context of this situation? In view of that knowledge, what is the best course of action? God never operates in random longsuffering – His longsuffering has purpose.

Ultimately, longsuffering is the empowering balm of healing to us. Colossians 3:12-13 "Therefore, as the elect of God, holy and beloved, put on tender mercies, kindness, humbleness of mind, meekness, longsuffering; bearing with one another, and forgiving one another, if anyone has a complaint against another; even as Christ forgave you, so you must also do." We express our love to God by forgiving because we are forgiven and that liberates us to operate in the situation in God-love. Ephesians 4:30-32. In the manifestation of longsuffering as the Fruit of the Spirit, we express merciful patience with people who we have received from God. By doing this, we very tangibly show to others the mercy of God and become an advertisement for Him. This creates desire to know this manifested Fruit by those who suffer with the dysfunctions of emotions caused by the marring effect of wrong thinking.

Copy God.

1 Peter 3:20 "who formerly were disobedient, when once the longsuffering of God waited in the days of Noah, while the ark was being prepared, in which a few, that is, eight souls, were saved through water." This is a clear example of God's 'makrothumia,' His 'mercy driven patience', toward people. **God waited 120 years while Noah preached the word and built the ark before flooding the world and gave a rainbow to show He will never do this again.** What prompted God's patience? 2 Peter 3:9, 15 shows that mercy prompts God's patience. **God's patience means redemption, a return to wholeness. The essence of this biblical word for patience is the delaying of judgment.** This applies to us as we manifest longsuffering in our relationships. We too, operate in mercy driven patience, delaying judgment so we can see the person and relationship brought to wholeness.

Ephesians 4:2-3 "with all lowliness and gentleness, with longsuffering, bearing with one another in love, endeavouring to keep the unity of the Spirit in the bond of peace." **This**

powerful manifestation of the Fruit of the Spirit fuels relationships and enables us to bring beauty for ashes in relationships or interactions. Even the most wholesome relationships go through hard times or growth cycles that require longsuffering. It takes emotional intelligence to govern our responses in our interactions with others. Very often that will have a healthy dose of longsuffering. Any married couple, or family member, or work colleague, or church fellowship member or close friend will know there are times when you just have to act in longsuffering in the relationship dynamic.

People and relationships can be trying, that's just the reality of living. You'll encounter and have to deal with all kinds of people in all kinds of situations. **Longsuffering is the training ground for developing emotionally so that you can have the right response in every situation.** For example, the way you deal with a difficult person in the Fruit through longsuffering will require different emotional and thinking responses to dealing with a child. This is why it is so important to develop emotional intelligence and have a good understanding of your own mental wiring and core beliefs.

Emotional Intelligence is developed throughout life and it impacts all your doing and being. You can grow smarter and better by choosing to and learning how. This is a good place to look at what it means to be emotionally intelligent and how that folds into the Fruit of longsuffering.

Intelligent longsuffering.

IQ is not an accurate measure of intelligence. Your Emotional Intelligence is. EQ is your 'street smarts'. It consists of 5 areas:

-Self-awareness - understand your moods and drives, be

comfortable with your own thoughts and emotions and understand how they impact on others. You understand your motivations and what pushes your buttons and in longsuffering you use the knowledge about yourself to ensure that your impact on others is transforming and based in the Fruit.

-Self-regulation - being able to control and manage your impulses and emotions. Able to suspend judgement, acting rashly or without caution. Thinking before acting. In longsuffering, self-awareness helps you stay even keel in yourself when dealing with others and toning your responses to the person for best results in relating.

-Internal Motivation - A passion for what you do beyond the money or status. This leads to sustained motivation, clear decision making and a better understanding of aims. In longsuffering, this translates into you considering how your goals and passions impact others and how to sustain your motivation in the midst of dealing with others.

-Empathy - Understanding your own emotions as well as understanding and reacting to the emotions of others. In the understanding of other people's emotional make-up, you use the skill of treating them according to their emotional reactions.

-Social Skill - Social skills are more than just being friendly. It's 'friendliness with a purpose', meaning everyone is treated politely and with respect. This is a powerful tool for transforming even the difficult people and relationships in your life. And for all your other relationships, you have an ability to find common ground, build rapport and manage relationships by using God's approach to longsuffering.

The intent behind this, as with all the manifestations

of the Fruit, is to bring all the goodness and power of God and His kingdom into each and every relational encounter.

This is a good place for you to assess how you operate in the 5 areas of EQ. As we all have blind spots about ourselves, I suggest one of the free online EQ tests to get a good, unbiased assessment of yourself. How does what you discovered in the test affect your relationships? How will you change the areas where you need growth?

Find an online EQ assessment and take it now…

Take time in prayer and thinking and write down what you've discovered. How do you need to change to be able to better relate with your spouse, your boss, your child, the stranger? What emotional responses do you need to cultivate and strengthen in your relationships to be more like God?

Find the pattern.

To be effective in longsuffering we also need to understand patterns in relationships. God works in patterns. He uses the patterns to confirm Himself and His Word in a tangible way and to assist us to move within those patterns. Whenever we try to operate something outside the pattern and timing of God, it aborts. Everything works according to the pattern and timing God has already established. If we try to harvest before the due season set in place by the pattern, we won't receive a healthy fruit. It will be sour and underdeveloped.

This understanding helps us cultivate longsuffering intelligently. By understanding the pattern in the situation that you are dealing with, you are able to assess if you are operating within the pattern of that relationship. **How you**

relate, the level of intimacy, how you communicate vary from relationship to relationship. You act and respond differently to your bosom buddy of a lifetime when you operate in longsuffering than if you're dealing with a stranger. Your language, actions and solutions will most probably differ. **By understanding this, you won't grow weary or give up or over-react in a relational encounter. It also safeguards both parties from encroaching on healthy boundaries.**

Longsuffering works to a different pattern at a place of work in contrast to dealing with believers in the church. However, certain tools work in all situations. Because the Fruit of the Spirit works Spirit to mind, we can approach a situation with, for example, a difficult fellow believer thoughtfully by considering which psychological tools we can use in exercising our longsuffering. How can we communicate with this person taking into consideration their personality, mental wiring and circumstances? How will we approach this and what will we do in longsuffering and self-restraint before proceeding to action or strong response?

Mercy driven patience keeps the unity of the Spirit and drives the manifestation of the Fruit. Using the same pattern of mercy driven patience that God uses with us, we ensure that our interactions keep the big picture in mind. This applies to any relational situation.

It's important to clarify one point: in situations of physical, mental or sexual abuse, we are not called to be longsuffering. That would be perverting the Fruit's purpose. All the Fruit work together, and that includes a zeal for right, as we'll see. We are never expected to submit to forms of abuse in longsuffering. Your body is a temple, your heart and mind is God's and is precious to Him. Having said that…

To get the gain...

There are times you will have people in your life that require a great deal of longsuffering on your part that you know you should cultivate. I'm not talking about abusive people, we've dealt with that. Just people who rub a little, take you out of your comfort zone, irritate you – the people you want to show your tail-lights to. They're placed in your life to grow you, and in taking time and operating in longsuffering by moving beyond your initial inclination, you will find great treasures in getting to know them. **Longsuffering is one of the greatest growing manifestations of the Fruit because every situation you operate in longsuffering you are acting beyond your normal behaviour pattern.** You have to grow and think to be effective.

Now, when you meet someone and you have warning bells going off in your heart or your head, do heed that. We don't have to endanger our lives to grow longsuffering, we have plenty of opportunities every day! By having a strong prayer life and knowing how to have quiet time to connect and sensitise to the Spirit, you will be able to judge each situation by 'checking in' with the Spirit. **If the Spirit says 'back away' turn tail and run as fast as you can!**

In the church...

Longsuffering works powerfully in the Body of Christ to bring about the opportunities and harvest of the Gospel. 2 Timothy 3:10 "...you have carefully followed my doctrine, manner of life, purpose, faith, longsuffering, love, perseverance..." It works within our 'of one mind' congregational life to ensure offenses and petty disputes don't pollute the power we have in one accord. Let's face it, church families can be very trying, so, having the tools available to the believers to deal with issues is very important. I place great emphasis in training leaders on the importance of qualified counsellors as part of the church to help when a person or the church become 'stuck' and can't move on in longsuffering. (I've put together those teachings in a book entitled 'The Little Book on Church Counselling: Creating a safe place to bring wholeness and healing.' that covers this fully[2])

Colossians 3:12-13 "Therefore, as the elect of God, holy and beloved, put on tender mercies, kindness, humility, meekness, longsuffering; bearing with one another, and forgiving one another, if anyone has a complaint against another; even as Christ forgave you, so you must also do." By the very nature of longsuffering you will need to learn to let go of offences and forgive.

Letting go.

The word forgiving is made up of 'for' and 'giving'. It is a gift you give independent of the evidence of whether the recipient deserves it or not. **You are not forgetting the hurt or the event, but you choose what you do with the remembering.** In longsuffering this empowers you to keep relating correctly without harm to your inner world.

In any area of your life where you are dealing with hurt, your first responsibility must be to deliberately bring yourself to a place of healing. That starts with what you do with the remembering of what happened. You are not changing the reality of what happened, but you are deciding what you will do with the remembering. There is great liberty for you as you take back an area where something else had decided how you feel and think and how you will respond to the event.

Forgiving from the heart takes a change in perspective.

You take responsibility in the midst of your hurt and offense and cancel the debt at your own cost so that the beauty of God may work in the situation. We choose to take what we experienced and use it to redeem another from that ugliness in order to release their God-given beauty. You regain the power of choice.

You provide a door of opportunity for turnabout and restoration of the broken relationship. It's a commitment to the power of the beauty of God by doing everything possible to birth good and destroy evil. This requires thinking forgiving, not just saying 'I forgive', 'I forgive' over and over. That won't bring real forgiveness, it only focuses your attention on your hurt or offence. So, we use the power of God's ongoing forgiveness from the heart illustrated in Matthew 18:21-35. Forgiving is not a one-time event. In longsuffering we choose to continue in forgiveness from our heart, allowing it to be an ongoing, deepening, and quickening process in us. Offence free living is a liberating way to live!

The result.

Longsuffering bears fruit, duplicating what's in us in others. Living our life well and transforming others by the power of example. This is being a living advertisement for God in the raw, open chest of the world. Hebrews 6:12 "that you do not become sluggish but imitate those who through faith and patience inherit the promises." The writer of Hebrews is complementing them on ministering to fellow believers. This scripture reminds us that faith and our mercy driven patience towards others brings us to a place of inheritance of promises! God ties our inheritance of blessings (not salvation) to us inheriting all that Jesus purchased through patience. Longsuffering is truly powerful, bringing us to change and relate in the fullness of the kingdom. It greatly helps us to grow and deepen our understanding of ourselves and others and relate in transformational power.

So, now we know what we do in dealing with people, but how do we deal with life and situations in patience?

In for the Long Haul

Endurance (not a manifestation of Fruit of the Spirit) is hope based in respect to things or circumstances for a desired outcome.

Whilst endurance is not part of the Fruit, it very often goes hand in hand with longsuffering. Although longsuffering deals with mercy driven patience with people, we cannot separate the people and our life from one another. People form part of how your life unfolds and how you work toward living in purpose. So, let's look at endurance.

In circumstances...

Hebrews 10:35-36 "Therefore do not cast away your confidence, which has great reward. For you have need of endurance, so that after you have done the will of God, you may receive the promise."

This is the patience or endurance applied to circumstances. It's hope-driven patience. It's the Greek word 'hupomone' which translates as 'perseverance, endurance, bearing up under difficult things or circumstances' with the expectation of a positive outcome. 1 Thessalonians 1:3 "remembering without ceasing your work of faith, labour of love, and patience of hope in our Lord Jesus Christ in the sight of our God and Father."

Very often mercy driven patience will work hand in hand with hope driven patience in bringing about destiny in your life or in bringing about the growth of the Body of believers. **These situations require us to deal in longsuffering with the people who, like us, are growing toward something. We exercise hope driven patience while we wait for the end result of the situation.**

Endurance to goal's end.

Anything you want to achieve in your life will require a certain amount of endurance. Whether it be losing weight, building a business, going into ministry, finding your partner or best friend, or any other thing that you are working toward. You'll have to set goals and work at them, deal with despondency, motivate yourself when you want to give up and keep going by holding onto your vision.

Let's take the goal of losing weight and use it to illustrate intelligent endurance. Ever seen a 'wet paint' sign on a newly painted bench and touched the bench to check? That illustrates the futility of telling yourself not to do something. **Bring your 'I don't' language to play in the habit you want to break and then set in motion 'I want'.** Let me explain how you'll use this effectively. As an example, 'I don't' eat snacks after dinner because 'I want' to lose weight' replaces your language of 'I can't lose weight'. Then follow up by replacing the activity where you habitually would eat snacks. And if you feel like falling into old patterns of eating, make sure you don't have packets of snacks everywhere! Out of sight, out of mind. Also, create a one-line slogan that you'll say out loud to yourself and put up a picture of you at your ideal or near ideal weight. While you're saying your one-line slogan, look at that picture and feel how great it's going to feel to be that weight. Replace eating a snack with thermic foods (foods that burn more calories than they contain) or something that fulfils your goal – losing weight, like an after-dinner walk with a loved one. Shake up your routine a little by going for that walk or find some other activity instead of just sitting at home or driving. Every inch you lose is a victory! You're moving to what you want, step by step, in a specific area of your life and your wonderful brain is helping you create the habits to achieve that. That is enduring intelligently.

Part of endurance is the changes that will come as you move ahead in your life. As you develop and grow in what you want to achieve, you'll find subtle changes happening in long held habits and relationships. You operate in set patterns in your relationships and the changes you're making will spill over. That changes dynamics in relationships that may not be easy. When my partner and I decided to move to America to complete our studies and deliver training nationwide we had resistance. Why did we want to leave when we had an established network, a successful training academy and familiar surroundings? Couldn't we do the same where we were? All the resistance made it a difficult move and as a result, many long-standing relationships changed. The first few months in the USA were lonely and difficult, but a clear goal and the phrase, 'this too shall pass' kept us on track. We had 17 wonderful years of travelling around the States making wonderful friends and achieved our PhD's and grew in unexpected ways. Sure, there were hard times, but we look back on it with gratitude at our growth and the wonderful life snapshots gained in the adventure. Endurance paid huge dividends.

To endure or not to endure, that is the question.

Life constantly contracts and expands. We have growth cycles followed by plateaus where nothing seems to be happening. It's great when everything is just growing and you have evidence that your endurance paid off. But what about those desert times when nothing is growing, where there may be hardship and lack? **The desert is a place of aloneness, where in the wide, quiet places you come face to face with yourself and your future.** It's an inner test to let you find out what's in your heart. These times can be very difficult and humbling because it weighs those things you are enduring for.

God is performing a very important work during these times. He wants to know if we can be obedient to Him and endure in these times; or will we be obedient only when times are good. It's for us, not for Him and it's our endurance that will pull us through. These times aren't all hardship and lack. **We also get to know God in new and wonderful ways.** The desert times may mean experiencing new ways of provision from the Lord and new directions for your life.

Desert experiences provide new lessons and new experiences that only these times can teach us. **It initiates us into a new, deeper level of trust and knowledge of God.** This often spills over in how we relate in mercy driven patience with those in our lives. Just like Jesus, we solidify who we are and what it means. **It's important to determine when the events in our lives are a desert experience so that we don't end up enduring when we should be changing or praying.** Our actions affect our lives and the enemy works to destroy too. How do we know which?

Ask questions that can lead to understanding because in understanding you can endure. Here is a checklist to help you get started. If what you are experiencing:

is a cash flow problem or financially based check:

☐ your spending (are you living beyond your means?)

☐ your expectations are in line with the reality of your earning and your ability.

☐ you have used wise decisions concerning your stewardship of finance including supporting the Gospel financially.

is physical sickness or infirmity, check:

☐ your lifestyle (are you overeating, not getting enough sleep, smoking or doing potentially harmful things?)

☐ your thought life and emotions. Do you believe the worst, live in fear or walk in old thought patterns?

☐ your level of trust and faith in what God says in the Bible.

is isolation, loss of relationships, check:

☐ if bitterness or some other emotional root is causing you to skew your interactions/ relationships.

☐ if your expectations of people are fair, remember no-one can make you happy or fulfil you except you.

☐ if you have found the pattern of the relationship and interacted with that person according to the pattern. Each area of life has different relationships.

☐ that you love others and yourself and express that love as Jesus did.

is loss, damage or harm, check:

☐ that you are walking in integrity in all areas of life.

☐ that you are using wisdom in your life and dealings

☐ that you're spending time in prayer and listening to find wisdom for your life.

☐ that you are using business, emotional and life wisdom in your dealings with others and circumstances.

☐ that you guard your life, loved ones and possessions, using all wisdom and kingdom abilities.

Once you completed the checklist and established that the situation has not happened as a result of your doing, you can spend time in prayer to reveal any areas that the enemy is using to delay or weary you. If you're sure it is neither, you need to fall back on your endurance, remain resilient and anchored in God's love and get through the desert place.

The desert only lasts a season and is a doorway into a new dimension. Because your endurance is hope-based when you come out of the desert you will enter into another phase of life you are prepared for and well able to master. **What you take into this new phase is the deep, sure knowledge of a God who works in the desolate, isolated and alone places and a clear knowledge of who and what you are. That is the prize of endurance in dry places.** Hold fast and keep going, your endurance will transport you to your end goal.

To sum up…

So, makrothumia (longsuffering) is mercy driven patience in dealing with people while hupomone (endurance) is hope based endurance, putting up with things or circumstances for a desired outcome. Both involve obedience and persistence of the believer, but they describe different qualities given by the Spirit for different aspects of life. Only makrothumia is a manifestation of the Fruit of the Spirit and this patience is impossible unless it's expressed through us by God.

-Be patient and merciful in respect to people and operate in the power of longsuffering. Mercy driven patience keeps the unity of the Spirit and drives the manifestation of the Fruit. Longsuffering works powerfully in the Body of Christ to bring about the opportunities and harvest of the gospel. You will grow in your emotional intelligence and ability to relate to people and yourself through mercy driven patience.

-Endure and remain hopeful in respect to situations or circumstances with perseverance. Be aware by intelligently and prayerfully dealing with areas where you see no growth. Hopeful patience for an end result releases the power of hope into the situation and creates an environment for you to examine, plan and execute your goals in the right way so you can use it as fuel to help you endure. Endurance done right propels your life to new levels of success and growth because of the personal growth you had in enduring.

THE MAGNET THAT DRAWS

Kindness is the magnet that draws us and others into love's effect.

And it is in this power of kindness to draw into love's full effect that this Fruit is so transforming. It has profound effects that can alter the lives of those touched. 'In a world where you can be anything, be kind' is a life motto for myself and my partner. We apply it in our comments and thoughts of others and the way we relate. And whenever we've had to deal with difficult or obnoxious people, we've done so with this mindset: leave them thinking about their behaviour, not yours. It's a wonderful motto to fold into your life. It teaches you to be 'kindness aware' in your daily living and creates an atmosphere of kindness that others can see and will be drawn to.

God's kindness does this with us and it leads us to stop and think about how we are relating in that moment. Like that random act of kindness that's unexpected or undeserved that stops you in your tracks – it makes you pause and think. **Kindness has this unique arresting power that can hold the recipient of the kindness in that moment and touch and change them.**

This manifestation of the Fruit has nothing to do with weakness or being another's doormat. **This is kindness with love intent – it's not agenda driven. These actions of kindness bring about transformation in the recipient.** Let's look at God expressing this kindness to us. Jeremiah 9:23-24 "Thus says the Lord; 'Let not the wise man glory in his wisdom, Let not the mighty man glory in his might, Nor let the rich man glory in his riches; But let him who glories glory in this, That he understands and knows Me, That I am the Lord, exercising lovingkindness, judgment, and righteousness in the earth. For in these I delight,' says the Lord." **At any time we think about God's kindness, we are stirred to gratitude. That's its power, it elicits a response.**

The gifts of God's kindness.

Ephesians 2:6-7 "and raised us up together, and made us sit together in the heavenly places in Christ Jesus, that in the ages to come He might show the exceeding riches of His grace in His kindness toward us in Christ Jesus." God's grace works through His kindness and look at what the scripture says that means! **This is kindness as the Fruit drawing into love's effect – setting us in an environment where all the love God is can fully benefit us.**

The lovingkindness of God shows His tender concern for others. The emphasis is that this kindness is love driven. So, this kindness is not just a kind deed done to someone who has a need, although kind deeds are part of kindness, but an expression of relational love. It shows God's Fatherly heart. When we act in ego attitudes, God responds in heart attitude. **It also shows that God is fully aware of the ego-driven attitude and addresses it by showing a heart-driven attitude.** Look how God deals with this.

Hosea 11:4 "I drew them with gentle cords, with bands of

love, And I was to them as those who take the yoke from their neck. I stooped and fed them." The 'cords of kindness' was there to draw toward God. He healed and loved them even when they didn't know it. In living in the manifestation of the Fruit, we want to express kindness in the same manner. We operate in the Fruit with full knowledge and without excusing the dysfunction operating within the situation. **We're dealing with ego driven people in a marred and fallen state with a heart driven attitude.**

Moving kindness.

This Fruit manifestation propels towards something. Kindness becomes the magnet to draw into the vicinity of love's effect. Because our kindness is so clearly evident to all we deal with, it's a strong silent witness to them that they notice. And these are the cords that will draw them to a place where they are aware and open to the empowering of the Spirit and the transformation of redemption.

Isaiah 49:15-16 "Can a woman forget her nursing child, and not have compassion on the son of her womb? Surely, they may forget, yet I will not forget you. See, I have inscribed you on the palms of My hands; Your walls are continually before Me." The nail-pierced hands of Jesus contain the name list of the world. **Kindness of the Fruit of the Spirit draws to relationship and holds in constant remembrance.** This is an intimate and passionate burning love that pursues and will not relent! Every time God looks at the hands of Jesus our name is evident to both. We are never outside of God's thought or love.

1 John 3:1 "Behold what manner of love the Father has bestowed on us, that we should be called children of God!" The loving kindness of God draws to the vicinity of His love so that we may know His adoption and the depth of the kindness that allows marred humanity to be adopted into His

household with full privileges. **His love gives us life. His kindness loads us with gifts everlasting.**

How do we express this in our lives? Pick one person you know and ask: 'How can I manifest this kindness to them in such a manner that will draw them into love's effect?' Now go beyond buying them a bag of groceries or making them a casserole to something that will do this. If you're not sure, ask God and do what He tells you. It may take an unexpected form or action, don't try to understand, just do it. **This little kindness exercise makes you kindness aware and, by doing it often, will fold into your life as a life habit that transforms you and others.**

Healing with kindness.

Ephesians 4:32 "And be kind to one another, tender-hearted, forgiving one another, just as God in Christ also forgave you." **The nurturing or kindness of God is our healing and our salvation. His nurturing attitude towards us is like an embrace about us, keeping us within His love and light.** Christ's tender-heartedness toward the individual is the example of the nurturing spirit of God in Christ and His tenderness to all. **It shows how this tender-heartedness becomes the place of healing.** We in turn extend healing to others by copying the same attitude through thoughtfulness and reliance on the Spirit.

How can being kind heal another? **The power of the Spirit works in the Fruit with us to release ability to us.** One way we can bring healing is through forgiveness. We looked at forgiveness earlier but I want to add a point here specific to kindness. The Fruit of kindness draws us to love like God and to act in kindness. Colossians 3:12-13 "Therefore, as the elect of God, holy and beloved, put on tender mercies, kindness, humbleness of mind, meekness, longsuffering; bearing with one another, and forgiving one another, if anyone has a complaint against another; even as Christ forgave you, so you must also do." We put on, it's an action by us, so we can copy Christ in forgiveness.

If we retain things against another person, we ourselves are bound in the action. **By being willing to let go, we free both them and us and open a way for the Spirit to flow the transforming Fruit to both of us.** The result is that both parties find liberty and power in the Spirit and can then use their mental abilities and decide to move on into new behaviours. If you split 'forget' into two words, it becomes 'for getting'. What are you getting? **Freedom! Life is a schooling process. Mistakes are teaching lessons. You are here to learn, not to suffer so don't hold on to things that hurt or limit you.** Let the Fruit work with your mind as it's intended to do.

If these past hurts pop into your head from time to time (and they will), simply remind yourself that you have made the choice to forgive and let go. Replace that thought with a little blessing to the person who hurt you, put a smile on your face, lift your chin. Your physical change of posture and your conscious response to the thought has signalled your brain that you are happy. Your brain will respond by releasing endorphins that will make you happier and your subconscious will start working with your brain to bring about change. Now, initially it will feel strange, but you are training your brain to think differently about the issue and creating an opening for your subconscious to do something new. Your changed perception about the issue releases your life and allows you to flow in the Fruit of kindness.

Being a magnet.

Where can you be a conduit for this love driven kindness of the Spirit? Here's one of the opportunities I had. In one meeting we held deep in one of the townships in South

Africa during the days of apartheid, my partner and I were faced with a long healing line waiting for prayer. I always made a point of looking each person in the eye with a smile to create a contact point before praying. As I moved to the next person in line, I was hit by this wall of absolute hatred and anger. It was so strong, I actually gasped. A woman stood before me with folded arms, glaring into my face, hatred radiating out of her. I could feel my defensiveness rise in response to the wave of anger when suddenly the Spirit flooded me with love. He revealed that she had suffered cruelly at the hands of white people she had worked for and when she tried to get help other whites ignored her case. My heart welled up in me and I simply wrapped my arms around her and held her tightly. Her whole body stiffened and she tried to pull away from me, but I just held onto her as tight as I could. She suddenly went limp, and started howling and sobbing while I just held onto her for about a half hour. When she finally stopped clinging to me and pulled back, her eyes were clear, sweet and full of peace. The manifestation of the Fruit as kindness takes many forms and the Spirit will guide you how to flow in it. Simply live in this kindness and be ready to express it as the Spirit directs.

Kindness in action.

Mark Twain wrote "Kindness is the language the blind can see and the deaf can hear." **In the Spirit-empowered person it's a universal tool that can reach into any situation or touch any person.** Jesus sat at a well in the middle of a very busy day waiting for one woman. When He meets her, He shows kindness by revealing her need without focusing on her state. As a result, she and the town entered the kingdom of God. **Kindness in the Spirit never loses sight of the aim to draw to love so healing can occur.**

A man is robbed, beaten, stripped and left for dead. Three

people enter the stage of this wretched scene and all three react differently. Luke 10:30-37 tells us the third, a Samaritan, practised kindness. The scripture uses phrases such as "compassion on him", "went to him", and "took care of him". But the Good Samaritan went further than saving the poor man's life. He leaves him in the care of the innkeeper with a promise to pay any expenses that the innkeeper may incur on his behalf. **Jesus is teaching the concept of 'humanship', showing how kindness is the foundation to our humanity.** He taught that we must learn to move beyond relationships that are based exclusively on familiarity and intimacy. This Fruit of the Spirit dictates that our behaviour among strangers should have the same kindness we give our family, simply because we see them as human beings like ourselves. As a conduit of kindness we, like Jesus, can draw into love's intent. Jesus' life and death illustrates this.

Titus 3:4-7 "But when the kindness and the love of God our Saviour toward us appeared, not by works of righteousness which we have done, but according to His mercy He saved us, through the washing of regeneration and renewing of the holy Spirit, whom He poured out on us abundantly through Jesus Christ our Saviour…that we should become heirs…" **God's kindness appeared, we are drawn to Him and He gives us renewal through the Spirit so we can become heirs. This is kindness drawing into love's intent.**

The Fruit of kindness works from love and is the power of healing.

You can only love your neighbour as yourself when you love yourself. It forms your blueprint for loving others. The same is true of kindness. All the manifestations of the Fruit must work in, as well as out of you. Kindness working in yourself towards yourself is the well you draw from. **By learning to be kind to yourself in your dealings with yourself and what you expect from yourself will bring balance.** Take a moment and re-read the section on self-love, then think of areas you are unkind to yourself. This could be the inner dialogue you have with yourself or your expectation of yourself. **Take these areas to God in prayer, write them down and ask questions that will help you line up your inner life in kindness.** Every manifestation of the Fruit must be at work in you first to fully flow out to others. You cannot live in kindness to others while mistreating yourself.

I'm kind to myself, but I regret...

This is especially for those whose regrets hold them in an unkind state to themselves. Not all may apply, deal with those that do apply to you.

1. Listen to this emotion. Your brain is telling you to look at your choices and a portion of your life where your actions may be leading to undesirable consequences in your life.

2. If you can't change the situation, let it go. If you're stuck blaming yourself and regretting past actions, it could turn into depression and damage your self-love. Find a way to forgive yourself or at least make peace with the situation and let it go. What would you say to a loved one in the same situation to make them feel better? Now follow your own advice.

3. Make sure you are not taking too much blame. Consider the circumstances at the time that may have made it more difficult to make good choices, or the fact that you had limited knowledge at the time. Perhaps you had to make a quick decision without full knowledge or under time pressure or had multiple stresses going on. Factor that in and with that perspective, look at what you can learn from it.

4. Think about life as a journey. Everybody makes mistakes. These can be learning opportunities that teach important lessons about yourself, your ways of reacting, values, vulnerabilities, triggers, and also about other people and how to take better care of yourself. Learn the lessons and move on.

5. Contextualise what happened. Develop self-interventions to help you understand how much chance or outside factors played a role in your choices, versus your own actions. This will result in decreased self-blame and regret and help you respond with a new perspective next time.

6. Focus in the present moment. Stop yourself when you are in self-judgement or just dwelling on the pain and regret. Enjoy your life in this moment with all its imperfections.

7. Be kind to yourself and remind yourself you are learning and growing. Forgive yourself for mistakes and lost opportunities and focus on here and now and what you can achieve today. You have done the best, given the circumstances. Let go, be compassionate to yourself and seek peace. Learn from the past and incorporate new ways to recognise future opportunities and how to not repeat past mistakes.

8. Who are you? Look inside and say, 'What type of person am I?' 'Am I the type of person who has big dreams, or believes that dreams are important, and have aspirations that for some reason I'm not pursuing. Or am I the type of person who thinks my responsibility to others is most important.' Maybe you would actually more deeply regret destroying your family's financial security to start your own business than you would regret never striking out on your own. Like every other negotiation in life, it's about choosing the solution you can live with that will help you move beyond this point to wholeness. Spend time with God in all this and listen to what

He says.

Life is messy, we make mistakes and don't always allow ourselves the freedom of a life make-over. Why not give yourself this gift?

Begin by listening to what you say to yourself inside yourself and write it down, then compare it with what God says about you. The discrepancies you'll find can now be changed by using psychological tools or even considering counselling to bring you to wholeness inside. This whole book has been a testament of how precious and special you are to God. If someone believes to the contrary, they are going against God and His desires for them. It also restricts what the Spirit can do for them and through them. And so, fully accept that you are precious and special to God. And then the Spirit can do wonderful things for you and through you.

And be kind to yourself so that you are familiar with expressing kindness to others. Let kindness be the magnet that draws you to love that becomes the power to heal and deliver others through you. Now that expresses who you are to the world and your kindness becomes the magnet that will draw others into love's effect.

Curate your Personal Brand

You have a digital presence as real as your physical one that operates on the same principles in this book.

Kindness as your default setting in your actions and thought has amazing benefits. This mindset will make you the magnet that draws others into love's effect. What does that mean? **Your consistent interactions in kindness make others sit up and take note. Why are you like this? And this is the very reason the Fruit brings wholeness, because in living it we allow the Spirit to point to God through us.** Titus 3:4-5 "But when the kindness and love of God our Saviour toward man appeared, not by works of righteousness which we have done, but according to His mercy He saved us, through the washing of regeneration and renewing of the Holy Spirit."

Whether we love it or hate it, we live in a digital world where pings invade every moment and streams of data are constantly bombarding us. Earlier, we looked at the concept of 'double listening' - listening both to the Spirit and to the world, in order to be able to relate one to the other. And as so much of our lives takes place online, we need a Fruit-filled online life where we apply 'double listening'.

Branded for life.

We all have a personal brand, whether we consciously work on it or not. Most kingdom believers have a skewed idea about branding, thinking self-promotion is prideful and wrong and should be avoided. **But by not thinking carefully about your brand and developing it intelligently, you are just haphazardly creating a digital image of yourself.** This is what people look at and assess who you are, including that prospective boss for that dream job. You can have a dazzling resume (CV), but before you will be considered for any job of value, most prospective employers will check your social presence. It's the nature of cyber space that everything... virtually everything, remains if you've posted it. It reflects your likes and dislikes, and politicians and companies use it to categorise you and target you based on what you have posted. **You see, to those politicians and businesses, what you've put out there is the real you.**

Your personal brand shows your internal values and beliefs, likes and dislikes, your personality and lifestyle, and much more.

By building your brand you ensure when people hear your name, they associate you with the right kind of things. For example, regardless of the view you hold about climate change, when you hear the name David Attenborough you immediately think of someone who is consistently passionate and vocal about protection of the planet. What sets him apart is his kind, informative way of dealing with a very emotive subject. And that is also why his brand has continued and he enjoys such popularity among diverse people. **Because he's done it right, he can keep sharing his passion and people respond.**

What, you may be thinking, has personal branding got to do with the Fruit of the Spirit? Everything. Your personal brand can be a conduit for God's love to work through, drawing people. I'm not talking about having to preach and constantly show Christian content. Your personal brand expresses who you are by the content your post, the things you follow, like and comment on. It also reflects your inner values. **You reflect kingdom living and who you are as a multi-dimensional being living multi-dimensionally with every post. Even if you never post anything blatantly Christian, the Fruit should show.**

Creating a brand.

What is personal branding? It's the life-long process of establishing and maintaining an impression in the mind of others about an individual, group or organisation. Personal branding, much like social media, is about making a full-time commitment to the journey of defining yourself and how this will shape the manner in which you will serve others. Your personal brand should represent the value you are able to consistently deliver to those whom you are interacting with. Managing your personal brand requires you to be a great role model, mentor, and / or a voice that others can depend upon. Your brand should also offer value, it should enrich others. The majority of your content should be about things relevant to your audience's interests and the smaller percentage should be about you. Do you see how this brings the whole Fruit in operating on social media?

Every time you're in a meeting, a conference, networking reception or event, be mindful of what others are experiencing about you and what you want others to experience about you. If you look at businesses in the past, you'll see that many businesses carried the name of their founders and owners. In the days before we could google someone and have instant access to so much information about anyone, people relied on word of mouth. (It's still a powerful tool today). People named their businesses after themselves because they were, in effect, saying, 'My name (so all of me and my reputation) is attached to this business. We still see names attached to brands and businesses, where an athlete or important person endorses a product and puts their name to it. And we buy that product because of what we perceive of the person, not the product. In social media, you fall under the same rule.

Develop awareness.

Approaching your online life as a real part of your physical life you'd automatically 'brush up' some things. It stops you posting that passive-aggressive post when your spouse or friend made you angry, as you're operating your online presence in longsuffering. It stops you posting something unkind because you operate in kindness. What you post is uplifting, informative, kind, loving – it's Fruit-filled. Why is this important? **Because you're building people's awareness of who you are and what you stand for.** You're steadfast and faithful in who you are and authentic no matter what is happening around you. **In a fickle world, do you know how appealing it is to find someone who's consistently showing a life filled with goodness?**

Once you've established awareness about yourself, you have a platform to offer the gifts God gave you to others. This may be your business, your artistic abilities, your ministry, whatever. **Because you've considered your online presence and made sure it only reflects your authentic self, you've created a living advertisement of yourself.** Those who know your online presence know you are the real deal. **Now, what you say takes on significance and you can use your voice for the promotion of all things that pertain to life and godliness.** You also have the perfect environment to promote your gifts and talents. Your social media becomes an advertisement that will draw others to you to find out what you have that makes you so wonderfully different.

Develop value words.

Your personal brand can become a life chart for you. How? If you have a clear personal brand, you can ask yourself, 'Am I consistently living my brand every day?' You can make course corrections as you go when you find your answer to this question is 'no' through follow up questions that identify why. **This is a tremendously motivating question because you're not doing it because you have to, you're doing it to stay true to yourself.**

If this section has made you realise your social presence could use some adjusting and polishing and you're unsure how to go about it, here are a few tips:

1. In view of what you've learnt in this book, write down how you wish to express you multi-dimensional kingdom life to the world.

2. Now go through you social media, all of it, and delete what does not promote your unique gifts and talents and is not uplifting to others. How could you make your sites a magnet to draw others into love's affect?

3. Think of three words that express who you are and what you stand for, your values, and write them down. How do you need to change your sites to reflect that?

4. How will you use your sites to connect and bring value to others by promoting your unique gifts and talents? Your social platforms enables you to showcase your personal brand in kindness.

If you struggle with the idea of right self-promotion, remember, you have a moral obligation to share what God has given you to enrich others, God expects it. It's impossible to share without using some form of promotion.

Moving in kindness and affecting and changing the world through our kindness, we need the balance of goodness...

DYNAMIC ZEAL

Taking all goodness to infinity and beyond

It's good to do good and bring good to others but this is only a very small part of the Fruit of goodness. Don't get me wrong, it's a good, small part and teaches generosity and big-heartedness and expresses the heart of God. **Doing good is always good,** so we want to explore the depth of what the manifestation of goodness encompasses in the Fruit and the knock-on effects it has to other areas of our lives. What is goodness?

'Uprightness of heart and life.'

This is the definition of the Fruit expressing goodness. **Being upright in heart and life means that your thinking and your doing is founded in goodness which includes truth, justice and God-love living.** God is upright and we copy God. Deuteronomy 32:4 "He is the Rock, His work is perfect; for all His ways are justice, A God of truth and without injustice, righteous and upright is He." **It's pure, unwavering, zealous goodness. This is the nature of goodness in the kingdom and all eternal heaven is saturated with it.** Why?

Because all of eternal heaven is filled with all of God and it flows into all of God's doings with us. 'God is good' is not some mindless catchphrase to repeat in church. When we say it, it should be said with the full realisation of what that goodness means. In reading Ephesians 2:1-10, we see God's expression of goodness to us. Though we were disobedient v.3, God made us alive in Christ v.4-5. God uses kindness to express His incomparable grace to us when we were dead in our transgressions v 7. We are called to an attitude of kindness, and to energize that character into acts of active good. **So, when we say 'God is good' we are also saying that as His children, we have that goodness active in us and working through us. It then becomes a kingdom declaration of gratitude for what is and how we do the same.**

2 Thessalonians 1:11 "God...fulfil all the good pleasure of His goodness..." **God's goodness is often shown as His gracious generosity providing abundantly for our needs and benefits. But God's goodness is much more than those things. It is the very essence of God's nature - His righteousness and holiness.** In Ephesians 5:9, we see that His goodness is closely associated with righteousness and truth. God is always true and always authentic and the Fruit of goodness allows us to live the same.

Pure hearts require right motives. Paul said that if he did good works without love, "it profits me nothing" (1 Corinthians 13:3). Doing good deeds coldly or indifferently, or to impress others will bring no reward from God (Matthew 6:1-4). But when the motive is to "glorify your Father in heaven" instead of yourself, doing good works that are seen by others is part of being "the light of the world" (Matthew 5:14-16).

Goodness works from an upright heart, the right

standing in life and authentic living.

Jesus lived like this. Acts 10:38 shows "How God anointed Jesus of Nazareth with the Holy Spirit and power, and how He went about doing good and healing all...because God was with Him." Jesus, the Good Shepherd, did good with the anointing – through His actions of good He expressed God was with Him. You copy Jesus and live in the Spirit and with your unique gifts and talents, given by God, do good, nurture and grow others in a manner that shows God is with you and kingdom power flows through you in all goodness. We're not manufacturing good, we express pure, unadulterated good that is part of Spirit living.

We all know people like this. People who are good down to their very core and goodness just shines out of them. You see it and feel it when you get around them. As a result of seeing this God-like goodness, we are immediately drawn to them. You feel safe around them because you know you can totally trust them and you know they would never deliberately hurt you. **What an amazing personal brand to be considered as this type of person! Think of the opportunities this would open to you in adding value to others by sharing your gifts. Imagine how you can influence others through example to change and grow.**

Matthew 5:16 "So let your light shine upon others, that they may see your good deeds and glorify your Father in heaven." Living goodness has very definite characteristics we can incorporate in our thinking and live in our lives. Let's take a look.

Virtue Equipped for Action

As kingdom believers we need goodness that is both kind and strong.

The Fruit of Goodness involves a disposition of kindness toward others, but it includes an additional aspect of honesty or firmness in our relating with others that is meant to lead that person towards reform or change. The word Paul uses for goodness (agathosune) is a peculiarly bible word and does not occur in secular Greek. It's the widest word for goodness; **it is defined as "virtue equipped at every point."** So, our goodness to others contains in itself everything to fully meet every situation in the fullness of the Fruit of goodness. Wow! Think about that for a moment. This is at our disposal because we are of the kingdom.

3 John 1:11 "He who does good (as a way of life) is of God." **Goodness becomes a way of life when we are active in benevolence, when we cultivate a mindset to do all the good we can and selflessly act on behalf of others.** There is no way we can do this without the help of the Spirit because we are seeking to copy God.

Walking in light.

"Therefore be imitators of God, as dear children and walk in love…" Paul spends the first few verses of Ephesians 5 to contrast what we have in God with the behaviour of those who "have no inheritance in the kingdom of Christ and God". Ephesians 5:8-9 "For you were once darkness, but now you are light in the Lord. Walk as children of light, for the fruit of the Spirit is in all goodness, righteousness and truth."

This is an active goodness that is a zeal for goodness and

truth. This works inwardly, in seeking to submit to the goodness of the Spirit manifesting and working that outwardly towards others. Goodness works from the point of truth in us and outwardly to others. **Kindness and goodness are intertwined in a strong relationship, with each creating momentum in the other in our life.** Kindness is the harmlessness of a dove, goodness is the shrewdness as snakes - Jesus speaks of this synergy in Matthew 10:16 "Behold, I send you forth as sheep in the midst of wolves, Be therefore wise as serpents and harmless as doves." **These two pair up to make us both discerning and gentle and bring about balanced dealings in a marred world.**

Light reveals.

Psalm 97:11 "Light is sown for the righteous, and gladness for the upright in heart." **An upright heart 'walks right' in the paths of life and as a result has the assurance that light is sown for them. This means we can see the path to take, the decision to make and the way to act.** And beyond that, because we walk in the light we are filled with that light, illuminating our own inner self and radiating out to those in the dark.

The light will light up your inner life with spectacular clarity which is both joyous and scary. Joyous in that your being is light because you are upright and scary because it will reveal in you the places not yet touched or changed by this. Now, goodness working in zeal in your heart will use the light to reveal those areas in your life that are skewed. We call this a conviction. When it is based in truth, this zealous goodness will help you face that limiting thing in your life and bring you to a place of wholeness.

True conviction will not shame you or diminish you because goodness is its foundation. The Holy Spirit shows something through goodness and then shows you the way out. **So, true conviction always has an exit sign.** It leads you out to something better. The Fruit of goodness operates in honesty and firmness, being wide-awake in goodness so that goodness can bring a response to the person goodness is offered to. **There is a response to goodness.**

Faithful and fruitful.

Goodness produces results, and works together with faithfulness. To live in goodness means goodness is consistent in your life and the only way you can be consistent is through faithfully creating good. Matthew 25:21 "His lord said to him, 'Well done, good and faithful servant; you were faithful over a few things, I will make you ruler over many things. Enter into the joy of your Lord." We can only remain faithful by empowerment through the Spirit. **When operating in the goodness of the Spirit, and the zeal in us is strong, it's faithfulness that will keep us on course and prevent us from losing heart.**

As missionaries my partner and I saw God's goodness in protection, in provision, in empowerment, in signs and wonders. We saw His goodness change lives and communities and create places of growth and a ripple effect of goodness reaching far and wide. In our business and ministry God's goodness guided us, gave wisdom and empowered us to strike out in balanced boldness into the fullness of our gifts. We see amazing results in our lives as a result of God's goodness, it's a propelling force of good in our lives and it has kept us going in faith.

Forward in goodness.

We all like to be liked and accepted, it's in our mental wiring. That which is good, profitable or beneficial is not always fun, easy or pleasant. Bringing what is beneficial, not what is popular shows the Fruit of goodness working. Ephesians 5:9-11 "(for the fruit of the Spirit is in all goodness, righteousness, and truth), proving what is acceptable to the Lord. And have no fellowship with the unfruitful works of darkness, but rather expose them." In ministry or life, this is hard and can be very lonely. And this is where a good circle of people who love and accept you will pull you through and balance you. Because if we don't seek to use our mental abilities, balanced counsel and psychological tools we could end up becoming hard and harsh in our dealings with others and with life. **Zeal can be perverted and operate through judgment and frustration rather than love and goodness.**

The zeal in goodness must be balanced by good works, it helps us maintain an 'even keel' through the storms of life. Titus 3:8 "This is a faithful saying, and these things I want you to affirm constantly, that those who have believed in God should be careful to maintain good works. These things are good and profitable to men." Why is this important? The Spirit is dynamic and works in all good, expressing the goodness of God all the time and pointing to Jesus. **When we operate in "good works" – works that express the Fruit and reveal the kingdom – we stay connected to our source of life and power and show God.**

Let's look at some ways this works in real life.

Lessons in goodness from a Samaritan.

A man had been robbed, stripped, assaulted and stabbed and left for dead, as a bloody heap by the side of the road. Two religious leaders travelling in the same direction avoid him entirely and go about their business. Goodness is about to invade the life of this bloodied, naked individual to bring life-saving rescue. A kind-hearted Samaritan interrupts his journey to turn aside and care for this stranger.

1. Goodness involves compassion and extravagant giving. The Samaritan, compassionately pours wine then oil on the victim's wounds to sterilise and clean the poor man: It's an unexpected use of his costly supplies that he had no doubt set aside for some profitable personal use. He bandages his wounds then hoists the beaten man up onto his own animal, not worrying about any blood ruining his saddle and his kit that he'll have to clean later. Then carefully brings him to an inn.

2. Goodness addresses and meets a need to change the outcome. The goodness of this Samaritan doesn't end with his arrival at the inn. He takes care of him overnight. The next morning, he instructs the inn keeper to care for him until he's recovered. The Samaritan gave the innkeeper two denarii – two days of wages – to use for the care of the man, and on top of this, told the innkeeper he'd reimburse any extra expenses himself. He put no limit on the innkeeper's spending in his care for the man.

3. Goodness lavishly gives the most priceless commodity: time. Putting aside his own travel plans, he takes care of the man on the road and then continues his care at the inn - right through the night! Surely, he had obligations to fulfil and people waiting at the end of his trip? Yet he sets aside his own life and plans and unstintingly and generously gives his time to this stranger for his welfare. Luke 10:33-35

These three forms of giving done in goodness provide a great blueprint to apply to our service to others or areas of our lives where we want to walk in goodness. Take a moment and think how you can apply the principles in the three points above in expressing goodness in your life, your ministry, your business, your relationships. Ephesians 2:10 "For we are His workmanship, created in Christ Jesus for good works, which God prepared beforehand that we should walk in them." We are like, and act like God, we carry His image and likeness and our lives are fashioned for good works. But how does zeal fit into goodness and what does it mean to be zealous?

Zealous in goodness.

One way we see zeal manifest is in the expression of our gifts, our 'calling' if you like, that was placed in us by God. Jeremiah 20:9 "...But His word was in my heart like a burning fire, shut up in my bones..." Jeremiah is experiencing a lot of resistance and is highly unpopular for the prophetic he is declaring to the nation. He's despondent and has had enough and starts the above by saying he's going to stop declaring God. We've all been at the place where you just think, 'what's the point?' or we want to give up. **This is where goodness as Fruit kicks in and moves us forward – the zeal of goodness. All the power locked in the knowledge of God burns like fire in us and we've got to let it out. Goodness becomes a propelling and motivating force through zeal.**

Paul felt the power of zealous goodness working through him that caused him to fulfil his ministry. 1 Corinthians 9:16 "For if I preach the gospel, I have nothing to boast of, for necessity is laid upon me; yes, woe is me if I do not preach the gospel!" **He realised that it was not just about leading others to the kingdom but acting true to his own calling in zealous goodness.** V.17 "For if I do this willingly, I have a reward; but if against my will, I have been entrusted with a stewardship." Your unique gifting and mental wiring qualifies you alone to live your specific life and achieve your unique purpose. **Goodness will hold you in your purpose and move you forward.**

And action!

So, it works in the major things in your life like your ministry or calling and also in your interactions with individuals. We use zeal grounded in knowledge in relationships and circumstances to create space for the power of goodness. But it is always based in goodness and God-love.

How would we translate 'uprightness of heart and life' into living action? Romans 15:14 "that you are full of goodness, filled with all knowledge, able also to admonish (gentle love-filled rebuke) one another." **They have zeal grounded in knowledge so they can help each other to stay on course.** "I have written boldly to you on some points," **demonstrates to them how they should use gentle, love-filled rebuke in the church to bring transformation.** Admonition is a tool for growth to be used through goodness so zeal is balanced and pure.

Paul recounts his zeal-filled goodness as a compelling force to reproduce goodness in his life through his preaching to the Gentiles. And he reveals that he's about to travel to Jerusalem to minister and deliver a gift to them (v25) and asks them "through the love of the Spirit to strive together with me in prayers to God for me" that he is not resisted when he visits Jerusalem. Paul's zeal shines through in every word, he's doing good, expressing God-love, bringing correction in love, and stirring others in their zeal. Titus 2:14.

Zeal is fiery, dynamic, its compelling and can feel like it could consume you. This is not the purpose of goodness. The zeal of goodness is the fuel of goodness to lead to some restoring or renewing place. **True, fiery zeal doesn't consume, it burns away the chaff to reveal the latent, underlying beauty.**

Balanced zeal.

Matthew 21:12-13 "Then Jesus went into the temple of God and drove out all those who bought and sold in the temple and overturned the tables of the moneychangers and the seats of those who sold doves. And He said to them, 'It is written, 'My house shall be called a house of prayer, but you have made it a 'den of thieves''' **This is the zeal that is in goodness, expressing in rebuke to cause good in others, and turn them from wrongful actions. It should be practised under the direction of the Spirit in maturity, so the hard word or action is graciously done and followed up with love.**

Acts 18:5 "When Silas and Timothy had come from Macedonia, Paul was constrained by the Spirit, and testified to the Jews that Jesus is the Christ." There is a compulsion, a zeal behind this goodness because it sees the situation and determines to bring change. Paul's message wasn't received, as we see in the next verse and he responds in the spirit of balanced goodness: Acts 18:6 "And when they opposed themselves, and blasphemed, he shook his clothes and said to them 'Your blood be on your own heads'..." Paul operated in the balance of the Fruit, preached in the synagogue and tried every way to reason with them. It was clear that they wouldn't receive his message and he moved to another field. **And this is where kindness must balance zeal when we are in situations such as these. Paul laboured for years in some places under very difficult circumstances but was completely led by the Spirit to know when to move on.** It's a fine balance to learn, and the only effective way to walk in balanced zeal is through lots and lots of prayer and good counsel.

True zeal is wrapped in goodness with a foundation of God-love.

It's the powerful force that will give you courage to take a stand for truth even if you stand alone. Because it's wrapped in goodness you will make your stand in purity of heart from the foundation of God-love. It will also help you in the midst of the opposition you face to not respond or act in broken thinking. **The goodness that propels your zeal ensures that the works you do are Spirit based and kingdom promoting, always revealing a loving God.** We shine with goodness to a world groping in the dark.

Goodness is wholesome in allowing us to see things as they are, addressing things as they are and seeking to find a way to release this manifestation of the Fruit of the Spirit into the situation. Goodness is, well, good! Because of this it operates in good and has positive outcomes (even if not always evident).

Goodness, the upright heart and active mind.

Like all Fruit, goodness is active and must be cultivated by us. **In order to have the right perspective and attitude to the Fruit, it's important to understand that our minds will play an active role in the level of wholeness in which we operate.** The Spirit works through our minds and our minds are controlled by us.

Luke 11:25-26 "And when he comes, he finds it swept and put in order. Then he goes and takes with him seven other spirits more wicked than himself, and they enter and dwell there; and the last state of that man is worse than the first." This deals with the deliverance from an evil spirit but the principle of emptiness applies equally to the mind as the centre of anything. **Once the mind is put in order, it must be filled and that takes effort.** Passivity is one of the reasons that the warning is given. **The house was clean and in order, but it was empty.** Cleaning the mind is not enough. Delivering the mind is not enough. If it's left empty, something will fill it. Something fills a vacuum. It's a law.

There are several characteristics of a passive mind that help us identify it by its fruit:

-The passive mind will not exercise power and authority.

-The passive mind will not create the new mind through the conscious use of psychological principles to bring change.

-The passive mind will not resist the enemy's attacks.

-The passive mind will not deal with core beliefs, negative thinking and bring control to the overlay of the mind of Christ.

-The passive mind will not be renewed with the Word and will not apply it in life.

-The passive mind will not exercise control over the will and the other aspects of the mind and deal with the old habits and thoughts.

-The passive mind will not pursue destiny and transformation because it costs.

-The passive mind will not seek to transform others because that takes investment.

If you have found that you've been passive in some area of your thinking, now is the time to look at that. First, go to God and ask for help to move into your full kingdom living. Next, investigate your life. Look at the fruit of your life and your thinking and write down your findings.

Ask questions of yourself, like, 'Where am I not growing

or changing in goodness?' 'What prevents my life from being what it should be? Where am I not walking in the fullness I should?' Deal with any prideful area you find that has held you back. You can't operate in the fullness of goodness and the power of zeal it gives if you operate in pride about yourself. We all have blind spots and unfinished areas that God wants exposed to His goodness. **When you acknowledge the areas you need growth in, you create space for goodness to dynamically propel you towards change.**

Ask how what you've been doing has worked for you so far. If it hasn't, then it's time to use the qualities of emotional intelligence to grow and change to become emotionally smarter and more effective. Now, take some quiet time in prayer and listening and work out how you will put off the passivity and put on the new mind. What **specific** action will you take? If you don't know how to do this, consider finding a good, qualified cognitive counsellor who can help you move forward.

Moving from a passive, powerless mind to an active powerful mind.

God and the Fruit of the Spirit operate in a dynamic atmosphere. So, we have to deal with the passivity our mind operated in when it was marred by wrong. The worldly mind is full of emptiness. It allows in everything and anything that will entertain, fulfil the physical or promote itself. Now, our directed questions are asked of ourselves to invade the emptiness with the fullness of the goodness of the Fruit so movement and change will happen. **It's meant to bring us to a place of active change where we can operate in the fullness of goodness and see the blessings it releases.**

Tap in.

Being fully equipped to operate in the Fruit requires an active mind that is growing and learning how to operate in the power of the Fruit and the kingdom. 2 Timothy 3:16-17 "All Scripture is given by inspiration of God, and is profitable for doctrine, for reproof, for correction, for instruction in righteousness, that the man of God may be complete, thoroughly equipped for every good work." This shows the four methods God uses to equip us for good:

-We need good doctrine, versed in scripture and living it so we're able to respond within the full framework of God's plan and the Spirit's empowerment.

-We need good leadership in church and loving friends outside the church who love us enough to input into our lives for our good – even if that means speaking a strong word. Our relationships in and out of the church should be well developed enough that we can take this in the right spirit and act on it. Making good decisions to act on good advice.

-Good personal growth. Prayer, leading of the Spirit, good teaching, good emotional intelligence and a use of the psychological tools available all help us to course correct. If we maintain the right attitude, corrections will be growth points in our lives and help us to function effectively in all the Fruit, including goodness.

-If we are instructed in righteousness and walk in upright heart and life, we are operating in the right way within the kingdom power we have available. By allowing God to use these four methods to equip us for good we're promised that we will be complete, thoroughly equipped for everything.

Remember that love, joy, peace, patience (longsuffering and endurance), and kindness precede goodness. **So, lovingkindness provides the safeguard against**

misguided goodness, preventing it from becoming harsh and destructive so that the zeal of goodness can operate as a pure, propelling force for good in your life. To steer this in steadiness, you need this…

THE SURE THING

Faithfulness is the trusted steadfastness that we have because we have character and integrity.

In a world filled with uncertainty, faithfulness offers security and sureness. Because of our psychological wiring, we crave sameness and sureness. **But the world is constantly changing and God is dynamic, so nothing remains the same. In the midst of this, shining as a sure beacon, is faithfulness**. It's the sure thing in the midst of dynamic change. Trusted steadfastness works because we act and live in a certain way that manifests good character and integrity in all our doings, even in the midst of change. Not an easy thing to achieve in a world where worth is judged by how well you can hustle!

The Fruit comes to the rescue as we express faithfulness in living and life. **It's faithfulness that'll bring success and take you to your goal using your developed good character and operating in integrity.** It's the 'sure thing' we can rely on. **Faithfulness will assist us in holding fast to the vision we have for our lives. Because it's grounded in integrity, it ensures that in achieving our goals we look like Jesus doing it.**

When we yield to the manifestation of faithfulness, we assume the nature and character of God's unchanging nature. **Through the Fruit of the Spirit manifesting we release the fullness of the image and likeness of God in us - we become in nature like Him and learn to relate and respond like Him.**

God expresses faithfulness in everything He does, and it shows. Deuteronomy 7:9 "Therefore know that the Lord your God, He is God, the faithful God who keeps covenant and mercy for a thousand generations with those who love Him and keep His commandments." God extends His trustworthiness to bless and save beyond the here and now and makes it available to the generations to come. His faithfulness makes His goodness available continuously.

He is faithful and constant in what He promised and loyal to His creation. He expects us to give the same true allegiance to Him and those we encounter with the same faithfulness and steadfastness and to build that attitude into the goals we set. So, are your goals driven by goodness and faithfulness beyond just achieving for yourself? How can you 'spread around' your faithfulness into the lives you encounter? **Faithfulness operates in mutual loyalty when we relate. We can be trusted and relied on, we are safe and merciful in relating because we copy God's model and so is the other person.**

But it does go way beyond that. God is faithful beyond this point and these relationships to the future with many new generations. Solomon reaped the rewards of David's faithfulness to God. **And this is a very important thing to understand about true faithfulness: it goes on and doesn't just influence now.** Psalm 111:7-9 "The works of His hands are verity and justice; All His precepts are sure. They stand fast forever and ever and are done in truth and uprightness. He has sent redemption to His people; He has commanded His covenant forever; Holy and awesome is His name."

He extends His faithfulness beyond those who are righteous in His sight and in true fidelity offered His most precious Son, His best and most, when we were hostile and lost in the marring effects of wrong. **God held the long view.** We express the spirit in faithfulness in exactly the same way. **We manifest faithfulness to those who do not deserve it within a world incapable of fidelity and faithfulness to us because we, like God, hold the long view.**

We are faithful, loyal, true, constant, and steadfast to all we encounter, not only to God. In turn, we operate on the principle in the Spirit that those we encounter will manifest the same faithfulness, even if we think they won't. It's possible to take this attitude because you're operating from the Spirit. Faithfulness operates in the vulnerability of giving allegiance and faithfulness without any certainty that it will not be abused, or cause hurt or harm to the one operating in faithfulness. **This doesn't mean naively relating. Jesus knew men's hearts but that didn't stop Him from faithfully completing His mission.** And this is the right perspective: faithfulness operates because you have an end goal, regardless of what is in the heart of the other person. **You're going to express kingdom life and bring all the goodness to bear in the encounter in faithfulness.** When we follow Jesus' example, we may experience betrayal.

Dealing with broken trust.

Your character and steadfastness in faithfulness isn't diminished or lessened when it's not reciprocated. Broken trust hurts, and the hurt is real and should be acknowledged, looked at, thought about and talked about to assist you to come to a place where you can come to the point of chalking it up as a growing experience. This may take some time and you may want to relook at forgiveness and the other manifestations to bring you closure.

Points on forgiveness to help you deal with broken trust:

Learn to be as quick to forget others' wrongdoing as God is to forget yours when you repent. Take the attitude that everyone is growing and changing and see the light in that person, focus on the light in them. Thinking forgiving, not just saying 'I forgive', 'I forgive' over and over. That won't bring real forgiveness, it only focuses your attention on your hurt or offence. Use the power of God's ongoing forgiveness from the heart illustrated in Matthew 18:21-35. Forgiving is not a one-time event. In longsuffering we choose to continue in forgiveness from our heart, allowing it to be an ongoing, deepening, and quickening process in us. The Fruit of kindness draws us to love like God and to act in kindness. Colossians 3:12-13 "Therefore, as the elect of God, holy and beloved, put on tender mercies, kindness, humbleness of mind, meekness, longsuffering; bearing with one another, and forgiving one another, if anyone has a complaint against another; even as Christ forgave you, so you must also do." We put on, it's an action by us, so we can copy Christ in forgiveness. If we retain things against another person, we ourselves are bound in the action. By being willing to let go, we free both them and us and open a way for the Spirit to flow the transforming Fruit to both of us. The result is that both parties find liberty and power in the Spirit and can then use their mental abilities and decide to move on into new behaviours.

If you split 'forget' into two words, it becomes 'for

getting'. What are you getting? Freedom! Do what you need to move on. If you're finding it hard, work on 'parts' of faithfulness like strengthening your faith.

Because broken trust affects us deeply, if left unresolved, it can stop you from flowing in faithfulness in your own life. When that happens, you lose the power of the Fruit working in synergy in all its manifestations – very much like plucking out feathers of a bird's wing – it affects perfect flight.

2 Thessalonians 3:3 "But the Lord is faithful, who will establish you…Now may the Lord direct your hearts into the love of God and into the patience of Christ." **In growing beyond the point of broken trust, above all else, lean on God in His faithfulness and those faithful loved ones in your life.** Pour love out purposely to all you encounter in every way we looked at earlier. Just become a love machine! **Focus on and surround yourself with love, sit there for a while and bathe in it – love is a great healer and it covers a multitude of wrongs.** Let the wrong of that broken trust be engulfed in love and cover it so you can move on. **All of these actions you purposely do is keeping you plugged into the Fruit and allowing you to flow in faithfulness. You are remaining steadfast and faithful because as image bearer of God you have the character and integrity of God.**

And also, be patient with yourself and others and grow in your faith.

Faith builds faithfulness.

Biblical faith is an assurance, a certainty, an expression of the faithfulness of God. So we can fully trust. Hebrews 11:1&3 "Now faith is the substance of things hoped for, the

187

evidence of things not seen…By faith we understand that the worlds were formed by the word of God, so that the things which are seen were not made of things that are visible." When God speaks, it's a done deal. **This is not only important to help us rest securely in our kingdom life, but it's also the foundation of the intention we use to manifest our life as multi-dimensional beings. Every time you see a prayer answered, an intention become reality, you are seeing God's faithfulness responding to your mental and spiritual effort.**

Hebrews 11:6 "But without faith it is impossible to please Him, for he who comes to God must believe that He is, and that He is a rewarded of those who diligently seek Him." Faith in God is simply trusting and knowing that God loves us and has set up a system that is the very best for His creation if we will but yield to that. Our own ability to walk in faith daily is the result of Jesus' faithfulness. We approach every day in the sure knowledge that God's love and our redemption is safe if we choose to walk with Him. **So, our faith is a direct result of God's faithfulness. We in turn, must gain the faith of others by showing our own faithfulness.**

1 Timothy 6:12 "Fight the good fight of faith, lay hold on eternal life, to which you were also called and have confessed the good confession in the presence of many witnesses." The faithfulness of God leads to a life walked in faith in God and His sure and intentional promises. We receive a gift of faith in order for us to be saved because in our marred state we're unable to have the faith to convey grace to salvation. **Faith is dynamic, it has creative motion that is going somewhere. Because God is faithful, we cultivate our faith to move with the motion of God's direction.**

Ephesians 6:16 "above all, taking the shield of faith, with

which you will be able to quench all the fiery darts of the wicked one." Once we are saved, it becomes activated as a weapon, a shield, a creative force and a character builder. Faith must be cultivated. Once we have been given the measure of faith it's up to us to increase this measure through use. **Our faith expressing in our faithfulness.** Faith is so important because it's the foundation of pleasing God and the trust we have in His intentional grace towards us.

By strengthening our faith, we build faithfulness in ourselves because faith is an integral part of the Fruit faithfulness. Our faith is anchored in the reliable object of Jesus' faithfulness. So, when Peter calls us to be faithful in the things of life, he points to Jesus as the example for us to follow. **Faithfulness must show in every aspect of our lives.**

Living in Sureness

Holding true in the right way to steer a sure course to a good destination.

True faithfulness empowers and impacts every area of your life. Every relationship, every goal, and a myriad of daily activities in your life contain elements of faithfulness.

At any time in your life you are most probably working on some goal you want to achieve. **Living in kingdom faith will give the foundation for the intention you use to manifest your life as a multi-dimensional being.** As intention is a very powerful element in living successfully in the kingdom, we'll explore it later in the book in greater detail. Here we focus on creating the right 'background' in your life for the Fruit of faithfulness to be effective.

The best goal, the best plan, lots of directed work and activity, all are focused and directed through intention to a desired end. Your intention is based in your faith that what you are striving for is achievable, if you stay faithful and hold your course in integrity. Now a lot of things come into play that form the background to make this happen, and it involves us preparing ourselves to operate on a whole new level of living.

Convicted civility.

We are "a holy nation, His own special people", as 1 Peter 2:9 tells us, and through convicted civility we create a 'colony of heaven' on earth so we can live in our multi-dimensionality, fully empowered in Fruit-filled power. We look different and act different because we are different, and everywhere we go that is noticed. This is the result of our faithfulness in the world. It shows because we are faithful in all our dealings and interactions, including being good citizens. 1 Peter 2:13-17. **Being faithful means we are worthy of trust and reliable in how we conduct our lives both inside and outside of church.** We operate in convicted civility. What is that?

Conviction is grounded in a belief system. It's being convinced and convincing others of the truth of the kingdom. We operate in this conviction in a civil manner. **It means we relate in a thoughtful, well-mannered way when we respond toward people, including those who are different from us.** Not an outwardly polite mask but the full expression of God-love. **It requires from us to faithfully operate in genuine caring and commitment to our fellow human beings.** Convicted civility doesn't require an emotional response from you, it's being faithful and operating in integrity. You don't have to like someone to be civil and operate in faithfulness or integrity. This picture of caring and commitment is so clearly illustrated in the story of the Good Samaritan we looked at earlier.

But it goes beyond that. We "pursue peace with all men", while at the same time cultivating the "holiness without which no one will see the Lord." Hebrews 12:14. This is a delicate balance requiring a thoughtful and prayerful way of judging the issues of life. **By judging or assessing our own actions and applying the standard we have for ourselves to others, will ensure we are more lenient with others.** Do you see how this is a way for you to operate in faithfulness and integrity both to yourself and others?

Faithfulness – taking it to a whole new level.

God created us to bring Him pleasure and our faithfulness mirrors His image and likeness back to Him and that pleases Him. Enoch pleased God. Enoch so enraptured God that God raptured him because, though he was just a man, he chose to 'walk with God'. He showed faithfulness to a faithful God. Genesis 5:22 & 24 "And after he begot Methuselah, Enoch walked with God three hundred years, and begot sons and daughters… And Enoch walked with God; and he was not, for God took him."

True faith based on who God is, seeking the pleasure of His company and His presence. **Enoch's faithfulness rings as a testimony to his fidelity to God and his generation, and through it, Enoch fulfilled his life's mission.** His faithfulness to God is clearly recorded in his preaching to the generation of his time in showing the time will come when the faithfulness of God must be weighed against the constant rejection by man. Jude 14 & 15 "Now Enoch, the seventh from Adam, prophesied about these men also, saying, 'Behold, the Lord comes with ten thousands of His saints, to execute judgment on all, to convict all who are ungodly among them of all their ungodly deeds which they have committed in an ungodly way, and of all the harsh things which ungodly sinners have spoken against Him.'" Four times he mentions the word 'ungodly' in four different manifestations of ungodliness and each way shows a lack of faithfulness to God.

God's faithfulness fuels our daily faith walk. In other words, our complete trust, reliance and confidence in God makes us the carriers of that faithfulness to the world. Colossians 2:9-10 "For in Him dwells all the fullness of the Godhead bodily, and you are complete in Him, who is the head of all principality and power." Jesus was faithful in redeeming us even to the point of suffering and death to do so. **He is believable and reliable because His very actions and His passionate pursuit of us have clearly demonstrated His faithfulness.** Christ is the living testimony of God's believability and reliability. Through Christ, God has more than proved Himself. 2 Timothy 2:13 "If we are faithless, He remains faithful; He cannot deny Himself." The more we assume His character and allow His nature to manifest in His Spirit through the release of the manifestations of the Fruit of the Spirit, the more faithful we become. We become more like Christ.

Romans 10:17 "So then faith comes by hearing, and hearing by the word of God." Godly, true faith transforms character and 'pushes out' the image and likeness of God in us towards the mind and life of others. So, the progressions is: **God's faithfulness brings the way and means to justification, which in turn brings us to a restored image and likeness of God in us, releasing in us the ability to trust God and through the Spirit helps us manifest faithfulness to those we meet bringing about transformation in us and others.**

We either walk in the faith based on God's faithfulness, or we will walk in fear, which is perverted faith. Both are powerful and will lead in different directions in our lives: **faith will grow the Fruit of faithfulness in us, whereas perverted faith or fear will grow emotional dysfunction in us.** Is all fear bad?

Right kind of fear.

The fear of the Lord is a great part in the Fruit of the Spirit manifesting as faithfulness. It's one of the seven Spirits of the Holy Spirit[1]. The scripture portion of Mark 4:35-41 relates the story of Jesus calming the storm with three words. The result of this was that a healthy fear came over the disciples in acknowledgement of the Lordship of Christ over all creation and His ability to operate in the fullness of the Spirit.

2 Timothy 4:7-8 "I have fought the good fight, I have finished the race, I have kept the faith. Finally, there is laid up for me the crown of righteousness, which the Lord, the righteous Judge, will give to me on that Day, and not to me only but also to all who have loved His appearing." This acknowledgement that there is a weighing of your life is the healthy expression of the fear of the Lord.

It's a good motivator to keep short accounts with God and people. Use a heartfelt 'I'm sorry' quickly when you are wrong and clear the air so you can return to relating in love. Winning an argument or needing to be right can sour relationships and change the 'issues' of your heart to produce a life different to your desired outcome.

The fear of the Lord is healthy and necessary in our relationship with Him because of His perfect holiness and righteousness. When fear of man, fear of circumstances or fear of the enemy dictates our decisions for living, we have moved into the realm of unhealthy fear. **This fear of man, life circumstances or the enemy pervert faith.** Perverted faith is when we fear something and allow that fear to dominate or dictate our lives – it makes us believe and expect as much in the negative and destructive as we do in the positive. **When we allow fear to become perverted faith, we become double minded, unable to receive anything from God or to walk in the Fruit.**

One dark night...

You wake up in the dark, quite convinced something is wrong. Something soft touches your face and you freeze. You strain your ears and tense your body for action. Blood rushes to your extremities and you breathe quick, shallow breaths. Sweating and awash in stress chemicals coursing through your body, you realise the sound was just a window shaking in the wind and the curtain moving in the wind touched your face. Slowly your rational mind takes over and you calm yourself. You have just been taken hostage by fear in the classic 'fight, flight or freeze' response showing up as the 'attack, avoid or accommodate' tendency we use not only in scary situations but sometimes in releasing our potential.

When dealing with fear in releasing your potential into something new, remember it's natural to feel some fear. It's scary doing something new. Just don't let that sense of scary stop you from doing it. Acknowledge it's scary, plan, prepare, set goals, train, and do all the other things that will take you from the scary unknown into the well trained 'doing it and acing it' stage. One more thing, don't use preparation as procrastination. The best way to have an end to scary is to face scary by acknowledging it and then going ahead and doing what you've set out to do. More on how to live creatively later.

Let me spend a moment on distress, what is commonly called bad stress. Sometimes we should be distressed. If a hungry lion has just stepped out in front of you, you should be distressed - it's a normal reaction to a situation where your brain must flood your body with chemicals to give you the power of fight/flight. However, we have very few real situations in modern life where we need this, so it's good to learn to deal with distress when it happens. **In most situations distress and fear is just holding you in limiting thought patterns and responses.**

I worked as counsellor with vets and abused people who suffered the results of long term fear and stress. I found that even after they had dealt with the causes and brought change in their thinking, some of them would default to fear. Their bodies and brains had become addicted to and needed the stress and fear chemicals and they couldn't function without them. So, once we had dealt with their fear we had to deal with their addiction to the stress chemicals and retrain their bodies to function optimally again. I share this to show just how destructive prolonged fear can be to you and what God intended for you.

Anxiety and fear release harmful chemicals into the body that damage both body and brain, increasing the activity of our amygdala (fear centre of the brain), releasing stress producing hormones and neurotransmitters. Knowing this, let's address the elephant in the room and ask: What is causing your fear?

Name, frame and tame.

Unformed fears act as barriers to progress. **Fear works best while it's undefined because until you frame it you can't deal with it.** Acknowledge you are in fear and not in faithfulness, then ask: 'What am I afraid of?' 'What's the evidence for this thought?' and stay with the questions until you get a solid answer. Look at that answer, then ask: 'How do I change this?' 'What do I need to start/stop doing to make that happen?' 'How will I feel if I do or don't do this?' 'Is any of this true at this moment?' One other helpful question: 'Is it helpful?' By changing perspective through asking questions, you enter a calmer frame of mind, allowing the slower neural networks of the prefrontal cortex to kick in. Now that your prefrontal cortex is running the show, you're able to harness its powers to think clearly and creatively.

Question yourself gently until you get to the answers. Now you have this knowledge your amazing brain can help you to find a solution and the appropriate action to tame this fear. If you've lived with fear for a very long time, you will need to work on your thinking and perspectives to bring lasting change. In some cases the action you take can include a good cognitive counsellor to help you develop the strategies to cope. (If you'd like to know more about the subject of counselling, I recommend "The Little Book on Church Counselling: Creating a safe place to bring wholeness and healing.'[2]).

Let's do this!

When you feel that fear or anxiety is taking over, just breathe regular, deep breaths. You're releasing extra oxygen to your brain and throughout your body that will dilate your blood vessels, send more oxygen to your brain so that your thinking will start clearing. Slow, regular breathing signals to the brain that the threat isn't real, and the brain regulates the rest of the body to relax. Focus on your breath, it will ground you in the present moment beyond the fear response. Using this very simple technique of just stopping and focusing on your breathing in a steady way can be applied to any situation where you need to move out of the emotion you're feeling and into the reality of the moment.

-Next, ask yourself honestly, 'Why is this fearful?' Deal with what comes up. Take a moment to recall God's faithfulness that gave you all your kingdom benefits. Why do you think that what you're feeling or what's happening is beyond God's faithfulness?

-Purposely and consciously anchor yourself in all you have learnt about the Fruit. See the wholeness flow through your life and into the situation you are facing. Now reach up in prayer and ask how through the healing of the Fruit you can find the answer to move forward. Listen to what the Spirit tells you and act on it.

-When you're caught in a cycle of distress or fear, reach out to someone safe who loves you and allow them to draw you out of the place of fear. Having a good, long hug has healing power. Spending time in the company of a loved one, you initiate the parasympathetic nervous system to return your body to a state of calm. You have a vagus nerve that chills you out by telling your body to release acetylcholine, enabling an alternative response to stress and fear, so you don't have to go into defence mode.

Anchored in faithfulness.

2 Timothy 1:7 "For God has not given us a spirit of fear, but of power and of love and of a sound mind." This reminds us that we have the Spirit who empowers, shows us how to love and assists us in creating a new mind operating in the soundness of the mind of Christ. This, in turn, helps us to build a life in faithfulness, no matter what happens in life. Take the scriptures that will help you and comfort you and use them to move you beyond fear, keep them nearby and use them and the breathing and questioning exercise above to

rewrite your responses to life.

Fear prevents living peacefully in this moment. Living a focused life with a definite vision aids living peaceful days. How? **Vision is not only about destiny and future planning, it's also about a focused view of every choice and every minute that leads to the future! You anchor yourself in faithfulness, fully inhabiting and celebrating each day.** Knowing you're showing up in your life every day brings a sense of peace, commitment and love into your daily life. It's very empowering and will work throughout your life, no matter what.

Faithfulness in barren places.

Abraham understood this. He held unto a vision that God gave him that he would have an heir and didn't let it go through all the barren years. With no evidence of the slightest change in his situation to show that it may eventually happen, he stayed centred in the faithfulness of God and stayed faithful himself. We all know the result. He became the father of many nations. Romans 4:18. **The Fruit of faithfulness in barren places is the anchor that will help you stay centred when there's no evidence that anything will ever change.**

Faithfulness and expectations.

Between 1 Kings 17 and 1 Kings 19 we see the great prophet Elijah undergo a huge shift. He seems to lose his focus, faith and capacity for faithfulness. Elijah had withstood the evils of his day, operated in confidence in the miraculous and courageously faced 850 prophets of Baal. Enter Jezebel who vows vengeance and uses her enormous power to sway favour for her cause. Elijah becomes fearful, running away. Exhausted and so depressed, he wants to die.

What perception changed this mighty prophet into a man hiding under a broom tree in the desert waiting to die? **Elijah had expected King Ahab to respond to his prophetic utterances, leading to a change in the kingdom of Israel. It was a sound expectation, based on good reasoning, but it was wrong. Elijah was focused on what he saw as his failure.**

No matter where you are in life, you will experience times when what you expect doesn't materialise and you feel like you've failed. You expected God to do it the way you thought and He didn't. At times, the situation may actually go in the complete opposite way to what you thought should happen. It's frustrating, can be faith-draining and make you downright angry or depressed. But, like Elijah, you are not alone and God stays faithful.

Here's how God dealt with Elijah:

1.He sends and angel to prepare food for him, wake him and get him to eat. Elijah is so depressed he goes back to sleep after eating. The angel returns and prepares food for him a second time and gets him to eat. He is so energised by what the angel fed him, he goes for forty days and forty nights from that food.

If you are in a funk because things have just not turned out according to your expectations take time to rest, and spend time with God. If you do, God will send you 'food' that will empower you for the next part of you journey.

2.Elijah enters a cave in Horeb and in the night God brings Elijah to the place where he must face his true condition, which is his real problem. God asks, "What are you doing here, Elijah?"(v9) God is asking Elijah to take stock of what has brought him here. Elijah responds that he is fed up, he has tried and all he got for his trouble was a promise from Jezebel that he will die.

In the time you spend with God, examine what brought you to this point and how that affected you. Be honest. Re-evaluate how you see your ministry, your life, your relationships or whatever triggered this funk. God will show Himself as God during this time, if you approach this in authenticity.

3.God instructs him to return to his work as prophet and sets out the instructions of what he must do, including the call of Elisha and the anointing of the kings of both Israel and Judah.

God's single-minded faithfulness will help you to assume again your life in faithfulness. Expect great things.

Faithfulness is trusted steadfastness in us because we have good character and integrity like God and we use gentleness to live life in the power of calm wholeness. Let's explore the next power-filled part of our Fruit arsenal...

REAL STRENGTH

Gentleness releases the real self in strength, truth and power.

The English language is constantly changing and adapting, so some of the words used in bible translations don't really express in ways we can understand. The full meaning and expression of gentleness is a perfect example of this. Gentleness is defined as 'showing strength of character revealed in meekness of manner, responsibility with power.' Let's look at how the bible expresses this and then use modern English to understand what it means to live in the power of calm wholeness.

Colossians 3:12&17 "Therefore, as the elect of God, holy and beloved, put on tender mercies, kindness, humility, meekness, longsuffering...And whatever you do in word or deed, do all in the name of the Lord Jesus, giving thanks to God the Father through Him." **Literally, be clothed with excellence in character, having a heart of compassion, living and viewing yourself with a balanced perspective and relate in a mild-mannered way so you look like Jesus.** How do we translate this catchy definition into living?

Show strength of character in a mild-mannered way.

This is not a goofy version of Superman's alter ego Clark Kent, the mild-mannered reporter. Your character is based on God's character and we've looked throughout this book on how God expresses His character in creation and specifically, in your life. **Strength of character includes faithfulness, truthfulness, decisiveness, clear-cut behaviour and responses to others and following through on who you are. All these should work through your life in a manner that brings the fragrance of Christ.** That's the key: producing a fragrant life. You see, all the above attributes of strength of character can be exercised to a limited extent without the Fruit, they just won't be Fruit-filled so they won't have the same power.

The perspective of gentleness.

Titus 3:2 "to speak evil of no-one, to be peaceable, gentle, showing all humility to all men." Being equitable and fair in how you relate and respond to every situation in life is the foundation of gentleness. Let's recap on living a life in convicted civility covered earlier. We are "a holy nation, His own special people", as 1 Peter 2:9 tells us, and we look different and act different because we are different, and everywhere we go that is noticed. Our conviction is grounded in a belief system. It's being convinced and convincing others of the truth of the kingdom. We operate in this conviction in a civil manner. It means we relate in a thoughtful, well-mannered way when we respond toward people, including those who are different from us in the full expression of God-love. Convicted civility does not require an emotional response from you, it's being faithful and operating in integrity. You don't have to like someone to be civil and operate in faithfulness or integrity. So, your whole perspective is from this viewpoint.

Gentleness lived in this manner detaches you from

getting into the 'heat' of the moment and allows you to approach every situation including the ones you are passionate about in mild-mannered civility. Because of this perspective you allow your brain to function rationally and creatively in responding instead of reacting to your life. And in so doing, you are going to passionately make your point and live your conviction, but you'll do it in a way that will be a fragrant example of the kingdom.

The 'growth talk' of gentleness.

We know the power of our speech, it creates, and in a world of social media that power can be used to ruin or harm another. Purposely operate in gentleness in your social dealings and find ways to express the things you are passionate about or the things that frustrate you or make you angry through 'growth talk'. What's that? **It's using the creative power you have in speech, in your social media and in life in a way that will serve your cause or make your point and take it further.**

Because you operate in gentleness from the perspective of convicted civility, you avoid getting 'hooked' into emotions of situations or people. Your foundation as multi-dimensional being is in kingdom awareness, all of it, and how that comes to play in any given situation. **From that point of view, you can re-phrase your dialogue to bring kingdom power into your interactions. You show the same amount of passion, zeal, belief and intensity, you're just doing it from a considered point of view to bring the most effect.** You can now flow in the Fruit to allow the maximum effect to unfold in this place where you are giving your effort.

Growth talk used properly forms the foundation of intention, which is the juice for creating things in your life. It's also the grower of your relationships. The words you speak over your children or spouse or family or friends are all creating in their lives. And you are responsible for what you create. Matthew 16:19 shows what you set in motion will be honoured in heaven! Here are three simple ways to use growth talk in gentleness:

-**Be courteous**. Say please and thank you and teach your children the power of courtesy - **it's more than just words, it carries intent with it that creates.** You create a courteous mindset which will spill over into all areas of your life and be an example to those around you, including your children. In the simple courtesy of please and thank you, you set an example of God-love in a world full of selfish, self-centred action. You are showing yourself present in the moment and aware of the person you are engaging with and grateful of the action.

-**Speak life.** Fresh and bitter water cannot come from the same stream, and your life won't produce abundant kingdom fruit if your tongue is untamed or divided. **Your words are creating, that's a fact - you choose what you create through your words.** James 3:8-12. Create opportunities to encourage, motivate, uplift and enhance others.

-**Frame your thought life.** Take care how you use the creative power of words in your thinking. Your inner world creates and issues the life you live. Your thinking is creating because you believe the words you hear yourself say about yourself, others, God and life. Use growth talk on yourself and create some life slogans that you'll use to grow your life. Retrain your 'I can't' self-talk to 'How can I?' to bring your growth mindset to play in the situation.

Apply the Fruit of gentleness to these three areas by acknowledging just how much power you wield over these areas, deciding to show strength of character by using this power responsibly. This involves being present in your manners or the way you behave to others, your words and your thinking.

Jesus was the ultimate expression of operating in gentleness His entire life. As the redeemer with all power of the Spirit at His disposal to do whatever He chose, He chose to flow in the Fruit and complete His mission. Isaiah 42:3 "A bruised reed shall He not break, and the smoking flax shall He not quench; he shall bring forth judgment unto truth." When people strived against Him, instead of retaliating He withdrew and still continued His mission. Matthew 12:14-15. This is the ultimate example of the life grounded in the Fruit of gentleness.

Calm wholeness.

Gentleness, uniquely among the Fruit, offers us the ability to live life in calm wholeness. It's integrated living in strength, truth and power.

Strength and Truth, fully Integrated

Integrated living in gentleness allows you to view yourself from a balanced perspective and live in authenticity and power.

Gentleness makes you buoyant, unsinkable and flexible. Imagine a cork bobbing on the water. Now imagine yourself pushing that cork into the water as hard as you can. The moment you lift your hand away, it will just bounce back to the surface and float again. It remains unaffected in itself – it's the same before and after the action of you pushing it down into the water. Gentleness teaches this buoyancy in life because it's not based in how your feel about a given moment but what perspective you hold of what the moment is.

Consider yourself.

Meekness, mildness, forbearance and all the other expressions of gentleness are not outward expressions of feeling, **but inward grace of the soul** - a calmness towards God and life that comes from our surrender to the Fruit in our life in the kingdom. Usually when we use language about ourselves such as passionate, impatient, quick-tempered or hot-headed when faced with how we are responding it's to justify action that, deep down, we know are limiting. **Gentleness teaches us how to live considered lives.** That means that your thinking and your actions are so entrenched in the Fruit that you can express your personality and character in authenticity – **you act like God while being very much yourself.**

God uses considered thought and action before He deals with us and His considered action determines how He'll deal with us. It's always for our good, brings growth or change or awareness and moves us somewhere. **For us to be able to respond in the same manner, our perspective is to operate in thoughtful awareness – like God, we consider the circumstances, we consider the motivations, we consider the result and we consider how to best deal with it that would bring growth.** This takes being familiar with who you are, how you respond, the reality (not your perspective) of the issue or situation or circumstance or person you are dealing with, and a clear vision of your ultimate goal and how this can be used to further that. **You're still the same, passionate person, you've just harnessed your passion to flow through considered thinking allowing the slower neural networks of your prefrontal cortex to kick in.** That means that all the power of your prefrontal cortex is working and you're able to harness its powers to think clearly and creatively to give your passion pure power.

Titus 2:7-8 "in all things showing yourself to be a pattern of good works; in doctrine showing integrity, reverence, incorruptibility, sound speech that cannot be condemned, that one who is an opponent may be ashamed, having nothing evil to say of you." Gentleness must saturate all our dealings and relating. It's the maturity to know that we have influence over those in our sphere of influence and yet choosing to influence in gentleness. Paul was a great example in this. He rarely rebuked but instead coaxed, entreated, trained, prayed for, promoted others, suffered on their behalf and related in love. As a result, you today read his letters and study and learn from his life and grow because of it.

The power of gentle restoration.

Jesus commanded that we be as harmless as doves when we are about kingdom business (Matthew 10:16). Being aware of the ability we have, as a kingdom dweller, to influence, transform and empower the lives we encounter is in the forefront of our thinking as we seek to grow in gentleness. It enables us to fully respond to others from the core of our image and likeness of God. Galatians 6:1 "If anyone is overtaken in trespass, you who are spiritual restore such a one in a spirit of gentleness…"

How do we restore someone who has moved from the truth? Bring the fragrance of Christ to that one and copy Jesus dealing with the woman at the well. **Consider what you want to achieve – what is the end game in this situation? It's to restore that one "in a spirit of gentleness". Now, change your perspective of the situation.** Think for a moment about what you would do if this person was very sick at home unable to get out of bed. Probably, the church or cell leader would have arranged food to be delivered to this person, someone may have offered to vacuum the house, or drop the kids off and pick them up from school. A group would have visited and prayed with the person, the church counsellors would have counselled the family and the infirm person. No doubt, their name would come up in the group prayer in church. In this situation your church would have a whole support system in place to kick in. **So, why don't we have the same system in place for someone who has moved into broken behaviour?**

Through the considered action and changed perspective of the situation, we focus on the prize and use gentleness to reach it. We want this believer restored in wholeness so we apply Ephesians 4:2 "With all lowliness and gentleness, with longsuffering, bearing with one another in love," which helps in keeping "the unity of the Spirit in the bond of peace"(v3). We restore to wholeness in love. My partner and I have seen the power in this approach many times in our dealings with ex-offenders and recovering addicts and seen the transforming power of approaching an errant believer in gentleness. This approach is simply looking at another human being in the same way Jesus looked at the Samaritan at the well.

The gentle art of having a balanced perspective about yourself.

We spent a great deal of time in this book on being authentic, living the true version of yourself, and the power that holds in the kingdom of truth. You have looked at your inner world, your core beliefs, and by now you are re-writing some of your inner dialogue and no doubt beginning to reap the rewards in your life because of your changed action. Have you begun to see yourself more in line with how God sees you? I hope so because it's the foundation of your relationship with God and will influence how you pattern that into your relationship with others.

Earlier, we looked at how having a healthy fear of the Lord is good. The emphasis is on healthy. In our training of leadership, internationally, we've often encountered leaders and churches that actively use guilt and negative talk to coerce members in the hope of keeping them on the straight and narrow. Of course, enforced morality doesn't work and the church moves into dysfunction and out of the wholeness of the Fruit.

God made you in His image and likeness, so, if you're taking the approach of 'I am but a worm' or 'a wretch like me' you're contradicting God. **Change your perspective by asking 'How can I express the image of God in me in the fragrance of Christ?'** You have moved from mentally sitting in a heap in an unchangeable state to being a dynamic kingdom promoter. Do you see how these two different approaches elicit different emotions and different responses? The Fruit is dynamic and always moves to wholeness.

Using your influence and power in gentleness.

On the other hand, if you believe that your anointing or gifting makes you indispensable in the kingdom or that you should have special treatment because of it, you are in ego not kingdom mentality. I was asked to advise one bishop in a charismatic organisation who was outraged at the fact that after promoting other deserving people in his organisation to bishops, he was now just one of many bishops! He called a meeting with me to find out how he could title himself to elevate himself so that there would be a distinction between them and him.

Gentleness is always God-love based and we know that God-love promotes, saves, enhances, bears fruit, sacrifices. It lifts up and transforms. Each of us has a sphere of influence at home, at work, in the church, in relationships where we can operate in our power and ability in gentleness. **It's just taking a considered approach to how you think and act towards those in that sphere of influence.** How would a carefully chosen word or deed change their lives? **My partner and I have made it a point to use our influence to promote deserving people. We do it because those deserving people are going to do great things in their new role.**

I make a point of spending time with the students to find out what they want to do with the knowledge they gain through their bible study. It's a way to make them think about it and it stops all they're learning from just becoming head knowledge. As part of the leadership in one church, and Dean of the Bible Academy, I ensured that one of the students in the academy was ordained. I had taught her for more than a year and knew she wanted to study to become a prison chaplain. She was already a successful prison warden and her conduct and my dealings with her showed her to have the qualities needed for the chaplaincy program. The only thing she lacked was ordination and I could vouch for her and arrange that. **By simply being aware of those in your sphere of influence you could profoundly change their lives, and, in the process liberate them into a place where they can profoundly affect others.**

Living in calm wholeness.

Submission is a foundational component of gentleness. You submit to the traffic laws because you know they regulate traffic and keep you safe. In just the same manner, you submit to God and the laws of eternal heaven because you know they are there to transform you and empower you. Submission is never about control or lording it over another, that is the flesh-based action of subjugation. If you have been subjugated, allow the Fruit of gentleness to work. Just like the cork bobbing on the water jumps back just as hard as it's pushed down, so the yielded spirit effortlessly bounces back from anything which seeks to push it down.

The difference between submission and subjugation is that the one empowers you and causes growth, the other binds you, usually through guilt and fear, to certain behaviours. No matter what your status in life, you need to have others that you will submit to. Having good, safe, knowledgeable advisers and counsellors and strong prophetic voices will keep you on track. We see David submitting to the word that came through prophets and Proverbs 15:22 reminds us "without counsel plans go awry, but in the multitude of counsellors they are established." Submitting to a sound course of action is wisdom in life.

You need people around you who can give you input. You cannot possibly know everything you need for effective living nor do you have enough time in your lifetime to learn everything you need to know. **That's why you surround yourself with people who are smart, wise, fruit-bearing and gentle that you listen to and submit to in counsel.**

Titus 3:1-2 "Remind them to be subject to rulers and authorities, to obey, to be ready for every good work, to speak evil of no one, to be peaceable, gentle, showing all humility to all men." Selfless humility is the aspect of gentleness that reveals we have moved beyond selfish ego driven living. This means living with all men in the spirit of humility, even the undeserving ones. **If we do follow through on living in the spirit of humility, God lifts.** James 4:10 "Humble yourselves in the sight of the Lord, and He will lift you up."

Humility pays great dividends and releases us from the snare of self-willed and prideful behaviour. It works with submission and a yielded spirit to set nations free and release compound blessings to the humble heart. No great revelation or gifting can function unless humility is pursued diligently. **God loves a humble heart because humility is dynamic and active. It actively seeks to do good and restore good, just like God.**

2 Chronicles 7:14 "If My people who are called by My name will humble themselves, and pray and seek My face, and turn from their wicked ways, then I will hear from heaven, and will forgive their sin and heal their land." Humility guarantees answered prayer, protection and guidance. When Ezra sought God, Ezra 8:21, in humility, he did it so that God may be lifted up as provider and protector of those who proclaim Him to the heathen.

1 Peter 5:6 exhorts us to humble ourselves under God's hand so that He can raise us up in the right time. **This conveys the picture of being under the hand of God and of using God's hand as both shield and guiding tool to shape us for the exalted destiny we have. It helps us arrive at the correct estimation of ourselves. We see ourselves as loved and lovable in the process of being fully beautified.**

Authentic humility keeps short accounts with God and man. This includes having a true estimation of what our actions and words do in the lives of others and understanding that at times we may unintentionally hurt or diminish others. When this happens, we operate in emotional intelligence and seek, with the help of the Fruit, to restore that person immediately, without delay. Simply put, we seek forgiveness from them, now. **The power released in a genuine 'I'm so sorry' with corresponding action shows the Fruit is working in us because our aim is restoring relationship by the use of our mental abilities in the power of the**

Spirit.

Teachable and teaching ability.

Your whole life is a learning experience. How teachable you are and how you teach others will play a big part in how you develop your life. James 1:19-25 "Therefore, my beloved brethren, let every man be swift to hear, slow to speak, slow to wrath; for the wrath of man does not produce the righteousness of God. Therefore, lay aside all filthiness and overflow of wickedness, and receive with meekness the implanted word, which is able to save your souls. But be doers of the word, and not hearers only, deceiving yourselves. For if anyone is a hearer of the word and not a doer, he is like a man observing his natural face in the mirror; for he observes himself, goes away, and immediately forgets what kind of man he was. But he who looks into the perfect law of liberty and continues in it and is not a forgetful hearer but a doer of the work, this one will be blessed in what he does." There's a whole lot of learning we do in this scripture that must then be translated into action. **If we do this, our teachability channelled into action will lead to growth.**

By accepting the word planted in us we remain teachable. It's necessary regardless of who God chooses to use as instructor (even a donkey Numbers 22). This has its own set of problems in how we view others and who we feel is qualified to instruct us. The best lessons are usually learnt through the most unlikely people in strange circumstances. Remember Balaam and Balak. We must remain teachable regardless of what God chooses to instruct, He will always use His word. **It's a very good practice to stop in the middle of any day and ask: 'What is God teaching me here?' and follow on with other questions to clarify and aid you to do something with it.** True teachability is characterized by an open and ready heart to accept that change is necessary and to be willing to make the choices necessary for that change.

Teachability causes growth and takes us somewhere. Circumstances in our lives will give opportunities for us to move ahead in God, to grow. The Fruit and our own mental involvement in this growth process helps us to develop a growth mindset. **We expect change, we make the choices necessary and we keep the vision of destiny central.**

And this teachability helps us stay grounded in the Fruit of gentleness. 2 Timothy 2:24-25 "And the servant of the Lord must not quarrel but be gentle to all, able to teach, patient, in humility correcting those who are in opposition, if God perhaps will grant them repentance, so that they may know the truth." A gentleness in being taught that stems from a 'gentle' ear ready to hear instruction, sensitively, creates a mature and loving heart. If we are teachable, we will have the ability to teach as is commanded by Christ in the mandate to make disciples in Matthew 28: 20. **We can only authentically teach what we ourselves do.**

Philippians 1:9-11. "And this I pray, that your love may abound still more and more in knowledge and all discernment, that you may approve the things that are excellent, that you may be sincere and without offense till the day of Christ, being filled with the fruits of righteousness which are by Jesus Christ, to the glory and praise of God." Here is the mature teacher displayed with all the qualities that must be evident in those who teach and those who are being taught. It's the prayer of every mature teacher to find the pupil grows to be equal to the teacher. The lifestyle of the teacher must be worth emulating in all areas.

Gentleness releases the real self in strength, truth and power and enables you to live in the fullness of wholesome balance. This creates the foundation and all the Fruit wraps up in this…

LIKE A ROCK!

Self-control harnesses and governs the power within to lead and demonstrate a fragrant life without.

Most probably the last time you saw a 'Wet Paint, do not touch' sign on a bench you touched it to see if it's wet. That's the nature of our curiosity and our bent to go against things. Most parents will tell you that one of the first words their toddlers learnt was 'no'. We have a bent to go against or push back.

This is not a bad thing, in the right circumstances. **It can serve the other manifestations of the Fruit, so we don't automatically obey because we are told to.** A great example of this is the apostles who were told by the high priest and the council to stop preaching Jesus and replied, Acts 5:27-29 "...we ought to obey God rather than men." Self-control manifests in these men, who have just been freed from prison miraculously, to not flee. Instead they immediately go and preach again. **So, the Fruit of self-control can grow in us to help us to stop some things or to do some things. As with all Fruit, we participate, use our wills, our minds to make the choices and follow through.**

The same applies inwardly, in our own inner world. **We often learn to operate in the Fruit of self-control in the outer things in our lives but leave our inner voice to say whatever it wants with no thought to how that damages us, our lives and our ability to live a kingdom life.** The Spirit of God lives in us and therefore we are a temple - that space shouldn't be a destructive, inner world.

You see, self-control must be exercised intelligently. Remember, the Fruit operates Spirit to mind, so you are very much involved in the outworking in your life. Your inner world determines your outer world. All your dreams, abilities, relationships and living are your heart, your inner self, creating the 'issues' of your life. Proverbs 4:23. You either have conscious, self-controlled 'issues' or you just let it happen and hope for the best.

God gave us self-control as part of the Fruit to train us how to live consciously.

It's so easy to just get lost in the noise and business of the world and just coast along on autopilot. **We fill the moments of our lives without connecting to the moment.** Why is this important, you may think, because I'm just chilling out and enjoying life, aren't I? **Actually, when we do this, we miss all the real enjoyment of today because we're not consciously present where we are if we're on autopilot.**

God and faith is always now. God works in the now because eternal heaven doesn't operate in the constraints of the time-tunnel. So, by always being in the moment just beyond this one we don't connect to the reality of what God is doing now. **If you're constantly crowding out this real moment of life that you're in with future moments you don't yet have. you end up never living in real time.** You end up missing what God is doing and truly relating and connecting to others. **By training your mind and life to take on each day in that day, really aware of what is happening inside you, outside you, in your work, your relationships, your life, you develop deep connections to your living.** Your quiet time with God is focused in the moment, so you hear where God is moving in your life and how to take your light into the world. This in turn affects how your respond to the day and the people you will encounter and how you will successfully operate your day. **Beyond your quiet time, being really present in the moment with your spouse, family, friends and colleagues is you expressing they have worth.** That will change your whole dynamic in the relationship in a godly way and relating then becomes a growing place for both parties. **All these benefits and many, many more happen because you choose to operate self-control and be present in your day.**

Thinking right.

Self-control is not taking cold showers to discipline your body or enforcing punishment on yourself and others if a certain standard isn't met. Nor is it denying yourself the bounty God has provided. Nor is it judging others because they enjoy their abundance of good things. All these and similar behaviours stem from core pathogenic (diseased) beliefs that need correction through the right use of psychological tools. That is a whole different subject that I fully cover in my book 'Create your New Mind'[4] and will veer us away from the central theme of the Fruit. But we do need to briefly address core beliefs and beliefs and how they affect your self-control.

We've seen that walking in love casts out fear and that love is fully transparent, it's always real. Allow yourself the developing of the image and likeness of God to imprint on your life. **Negative core beliefs stop development and growth in the areas they inhabit because instead of responding to this moment in this moment, we respond and live this moment from past experience.** What are core beliefs?

Your personal inner world, your beliefs that you hold about yourself, the world around you, other people and God all fall into the perception you hold and therefore determine your reality. The decisions you're making right now and every day about your life are based on your beliefs about your reality, and the possibilities that exist in your reality are defined by your beliefs. Many of these were established during childhood, with other beliefs left over from situations and circumstances that are no longer relevant. **Beliefs that were once useful to you to some degree, may now be the same beliefs that imprison you and keep you away from unrestricted Fruit-filled living.**

Your beliefs are at the centre of who you are and discovering what those beliefs are and how they play out and impact you and your life in either a positive or negative way is an essential part of your kingdom living. It may be a belief you hold about your personal identity, your abilities, skills or lack of them, a belief that you're not worthy, not lovable, not attractive enough or maybe it's one of the many beliefs you have about your financial situation, or something different. These all determine how you believe you should act, respond, feel or deal with any given situation. You know how some of these skewed thoughts make you feel and you've seen the results in your life.

Self-control to the rescue.

Your mind controls your life and right thinking is connected to connection with God, as we've already seen. Now God's already given us the Fruit and it's up to us to exercise the self-control over skewed thinking. We take off the old ways of thinking by exposing and dealing with core beliefs and binding thinking.

2 Corinthians 10:5 "casting down arguments and every high thing that exalts itself against the knowledge of God, bringing every thought into captivity to the obedience of Christ." Imagine seeking through a building to find any insurgents that have entered to commit acts of harm. In order to liberate the building, we go from room to room armed to the teeth to search and destroy. At each liberated room, the soldier yells 'clear' to signal that there's no danger in that room. We use the same kind of tactics to cast down arguments, damaging core beliefs and binding and limiting thoughts. We finally get to turn the tables on our marred mind by taking arguments, high things and thoughts that exalt themselves against God captive and clearing the rooms in our minds!

Your mind is your bridge of possibility, linking your spirit and body and enabling you to live a life of possibility as a multi-dimensional being. This extra ordinary gift we have of Self-control is the determining factor of how successfully you will live in your own skin. And the first place this is at work is in what you allow as core beliefs.

In dealing with this, we often tend to become parental with ourselves with 'musts' and 'must nots' that simply won't work and which then leave us feeling defeated. We are all works in progress, learning to walk in the great and marvellous gifts we've been given as kingdom dwellers. **By a simple adjustment of perception, we can, instead, approach our inner world in the Fruit of gentleness and intelligent self-questioning.**

Facing your core.

1. Listen to what you are saying to yourself and about your life. Ask questions of yourself, like, 'Is what I'm saying about myself true?' and follow it with 'What is the evidence of that?' and end with 'Is this kingdom living as a multi-dimensional being?

2. Write down what your inner voice is saying and your answers to the three questions above.

3. Next to each statement put the truth about who you are in the kingdom and what that means for your life. Start each statement with: 'The truth and reality about me is...' These statements are based on what you have learnt throughout this book and the scriptures that accompany each area.

4. Once you've completed this, write out your 'Truth and reality list' and keep it with you. Take time daily to read it and when you find yourself saying or thinking things about yourself that are contrary to what God says about you, say your list out loud. (Hearing your own voice brings faith and it's easier to believe because it's your own voice.) You are exercising self-control over how you will see yourself and what you will allow yourself to believe about yourself.

Cultivating a new inner voice.

You are changing old ways of doing things which is taking you out of your comfort zone, so you need to offer yourself support and encouragement. Whatever you would say to someone you care about if they are where you are, say to yourself. **Remember, there is no such thing as failure, just unacceptable outcomes.** Use your perceived failures as an opportunity to stay with what happened, look at it with an attitude to finding a better way of doing this. This will remove your self-judgment and allow your most creative brain space to re-invent the situation. Take lots of time to remind yourself of your abilities, your past success and the highlights of your achievements. Did you do athletics at school? Display your medals where you can see them. Win best employee of the month? Paste a picture of you with the award next to your vision board. Now look at that, relive how you felt, savour it and enjoy it. You are allowing momentary positives to sink into your long-term memory and become the inner strength of resilience and you are changing what you believe and say to yourself.

It takes self-control to not default to old habits in thinking and this is where you can use Spirit empowerment and prayer to re-energise you. Also, surround yourself with people who live Fruit-filled lives that show who will encourage and challenge you to do the same and grow with them.

It's good but it's not right.

Without self-control we cannot harness our passions and we end up destroying ourselves and drowning in self-defeat. Self-control includes temperance, restraining passions and appetites and harnessing them into fruitful, godly living. **We replace outward restraint with inward discipline. And discipline is nothing more than living a tidy life.**

Proverbs 25:28 "Whoever has no rule over his own spirit is like a city broken down, without walls." Self-control offers a wall of protection from those worldly things and those people that seek to harm and destroy and from our own unrenewed areas in life. **Whatever we don't have power over, we will be under that power.** This includes even those things that are not wrong. There are some things God clearly tells us to stay away from even if they're not wrong, and in these, we will operate in the Fruit to obey because it may not always be easy to avoid. Paul understood this.

1 Corinthians 6:12 "All things are lawful for me, but all things are not helpful. All things are lawful to me, but I will

not be brought under the power of any." This is a great key to self-control. We simply refuse to allow the flesh, enemy or the world to hold us captive. It demands vigilance and constant assessment to see if that which is offered to us, innocently or not, could in fact hinder our progress in the living of a full life. This applies to life, friendships, church, family and everything else. **By simply being present in your life, you can assess the things that arise and ask, 'Is this helpful to my empowered kingdom living?'**

Self-control brings growth.

If you want to learn an instrument you have to have self-control in practice and preparation and any athlete knows the power of self-control in eating right, sleeping right, exercising right and living right to achieve the goal. 1 Corinthians 9:26 "I therefore so run, not as uncertainly; so, fight I, not as one that beats the air." **It's just living with the realization that your life is not a dress rehearsal and that every day you have comes only once. The key is to enjoy your life, live it, grow in it by being present in this day in the right way.**

Self-control over the mind.

Psalm 101:2-8 shows the declaration of David to "behave myself wisely" by not allowing "any wicked thing before my eyes", and "I will not know a wicked person" or tolerate anyone who slanders a neighbour or is proud. **This is a declaration of self-control that David is setting of how he chooses to live his life.** He goes on, "My eyes will be on the fruitful of the land, that they may dwell with me, he that walks in a perfect way, he will serve me." This is a king ensuring he surrounds himself with the right kind of people so he can behave wisely. **You see, self-control includes our environment and what we create in our lives. And our thinking and our inner life sets the tone for our life, our** friends and our living.

Walls and boundaries.

The inner self also makes the choice over issues of control, mastery and authority of boundaries. God demands walls wherever He lives, and He hedges us about with His hedge of safety. Living within the Fruit of self-control means we set boundaries of what we will allow in our lives based on healthy, psychological principles. For example, being unable to ever say no to someone or something (even the church) is damaging to everyone involved. **Delineating our time and life is a form of worship as we are seeing our life and time as something we invest wisely and not waste.** It takes emotional intelligence and the operation of its five elements of self-awareness, self-regulation, motivation, empathy and social skills to operate in self-control effectively. By now you would have completed a good online assessment of emotional intelligence and know how you function in it. By using what you have learnt about yourself, you will be able to relate and interact with others in a manner that respects your boundaries and theirs. Self-control and the other Fruit help you to effectively achieve this.

Creating My Life

In order to have effective self-control over our minds and our lives, we need to assess the fruit produced in our lives.

It's out of the abundance of our inner life that we produce our living and relating. Luke 6:45 "A good man out of the good treasure of his heart, brings forth that which is good... for out of the abundance of his heart his mouth speaks."

Your heart is the centre of you, the control room of your life. **Through your God-given free will, you are in charge of what you allow into your inner world, how you process what is there and what that produces in your life.**

To do this effectively and successfully you use the power of self-control to pause, stop, listen, look, decide, change, speak and grow.

Self-control to pause.

The Fruit will empower you through the Spirit to stop things you recognise as harmful to yourself. But before you can fully assess that, you have to stop and take stock. That's easier said than done. You have to purposely create space to do this. When I was counselling, it was usually at this point that the person in front of me would say, 'I don't have time to do this! Do you know how busy I am?' Newsflash. We all have busy lives. By just not checking social media endlessly someone could gain an hour or more a day, that will free up about 7 hours in a week – more than enough time to assess their life and really look at the areas they're not happy with. You have control over your time options and prioritisation.

What you're deciding at this point is if you want to invest your time (which is your life) or spend it. How has doing what you're doing in and with your life been working out for you so far? **Change starts with awareness.** Awareness requires you to create the space in your life to assess the fruit of your life. By using the self-control to use your time for something that will grow your life, you can have this time to pause and assess. You will still be able to do all your other activities. Once you start controlling your time, you're going to find you do a whole lot more real living. You have time to pause and appreciate your life, look at it, find joy in the great parts and be aware of the parts that aren't working. **The self-**

control to pause and see what fruit your life is producing brings gratitude for what is working and awareness of what is not.

Self-control to stop.

Knowing what doesn't work gives you a framework or an area that needs your specific attention. **You have to show the self-control to stop and take the time to decide what you need to do to change this.** Knowing and framing an area in your life to work better and doing something about it is what separates out those who will use the Fruit of self-control and those who won't. So, once you've stopped to look at what you've discovered, ask yourself the hard questions that will give you an understanding of why you do it and how to stop.

It's no good passionately declaring that you're going to stop, you need to understand why you do things, why you've kept doing it even when it makes you unhappy, and what your triggers are that make you do it. Stop, and really think about this. Ask questions of yourself, use some of your quiet time to talk to God about it. Stop in the space you have created and listen, respond and apply. Remember, this is about more than just letting go of something that makes you unfulfilled or unhappy, it's about fleshing out kingdom life into destiny. If you struggle with this, consider a good counsellor or read my book, 'The Bridge of Possibility: How to link the physical and the spiritual to release your destiny'[3]

Self-control to listen.

Ever been in the company of someone who just keeps talking and never hears a word of what you're saying? You know how your brain and body responds to people like that. Your brain is the amazing biological circuitry that connects you to your incredible mind to work in concert in producing your life. When you never stop to listen to your own inner dialogue and you just let it motor mouth on, your brain responds in the same way it did to that person who never stops talking.

God hard-wired you to need times of quiet in mind and mouth. In Psalm 46:10 "Be still and know that I am God" means quietness, relaxing, withdrawing and sinking down. I like this. **It's so much more than quietening the mind and mouth, it's a letting go and opening up the space in which to hear and experience God and eternal heaven.** You can sink down into all of God and just sit there and allow your life to be saturated by all the good of eternal heaven. When you return to your normal activities you'll bring that back with you.

Here's an easy way to help you cultivate the habit of listening. Take 5 minutes, just sit quietly and breathe and smile. Put your focus on your breathing, feel where you can feel that breath, follow it all the way down and back up. That's all, just breathe and smile. You have the most intuitive brain, constantly accommodating millions of micro impulses. The two actions of breathing and smiling will relax you and help you focus happily in the moment where your creative brain can create. Focused breathing improves emotional and brain function. You breathe all the time; all you'll do differently is being aware of it. Science shows that having focused attention on the breath changes grey matter in the brain, so you're helping your brain form new neural paths and breaking negative behaviours, win-win! Because you are present in the moment you can listen to yourself and God in an attentive way that will give you the full picture of what God is saying and what you should do.

Self-control to look.

We avoid seepage into our redeemed spirit by making sure the things we put in front of our eyes won't pollute our minds and lives. Looking at things, activities, relationships and habits in our lives is the next step in applying self-control. Now it's easy to get into excuses of why we have allowed these things in our lives, and I've even had some clients in counselling misquoting scripture to back up a dysfunction. God expects us to be open to look at our lives and hearts and make sure we are 'issuing' a wonderful life. Psalm 139:23 "Search me, O God, and know my heart; Try me, and know my thoughts..." is a weighing of ourselves, a looking that shows the reality of what we are about.

God looks and finds the right heart when we have taken time to look and grow. Imagine you are a building inspector sent to see if a dwelling is up to code, fit to be inhabited and a safe environment. **It's a dispassionate assessment with a specific purpose: Is the dwelling a fit place.** If you take this attitude in your looking and assessing of your life, your excuses become irrelevant because the purpose of your looking is to inspect and make this a happy, safe, beautiful dwelling – a place fit for a king's kid.

When my partner and I knew we would be moving to England, we sat down and compiled a list of 37 criteria for the area we would live in. We figured that as we were going through the stress of an international move we wanted the perfect environment to move to. These included living at the coast, clean air, surrounded by natural beauty and wildlife, historical interesting area, architecture etc. We had no idea where that area would be in England but we knew that's where we wanted to live. The first thing we did was change our screen savers on our computers to beautiful coastal scenes so every time we looked at our computers we were affirming what we wanted. We also used visualised intention and prayer to hold it before our inner eye until we left

America. A week after writing our criteria and changing our screens, quite casually, an area was mentioned in a TV show and we realised we hadn't looked at that as a potential area, so we googled it. Everything we saw about it ticked our 37 criteria. Once we arrived in London, we took a day trip to the area and knew it was home from the moment we stepped off the ferry and we've never looked back. **Looking in self-control is not only avoiding some things but using the power of vision to create your life consciously.**

Self-control to decide.

The great truth about our lives is that we make the ultimate choices that govern the direction of our lives. **The decisions you make will fuel your actions that will produce your life.** This is where the rubber hits the road. You're going to take actions based on the power and soundness of what you decide so, making the right decisions with the right perspective in the power of the Fruit is of great importance.

Many people hesitate here. 'What if I make the wrong decisions?' Let's examine what decision means. **When you decide you are making a judgment or determining a preference or coming to a conclusion about a matter.** You do this on the evidence available to achieve an envisioned end result. **So, although your decision to change remains unchanged how the changes happen will evolve as you grow and change.** Self-control keeps you in a growth mindset to keep growing as a kingdom dweller while staying fluid in how you exercise that self-control when you get down to the nitty gritty. Let's say you want to become a research scientist. You would need to operate self-control in studying in your field, putting in the hours and making the sacrifices to qualify. Once you're qualified, your self-control will make sure you stay up to date with new developments as you research in your field. You would have to follow the scientific protocols and discipline in your research and continue to grow and change as your research progresses. **So, self-control is both cast in stone and totally fluid at the same time.**

Consistently maintain self-control in living as a kingdom believer, and remain fluid in how you apply self-control to live a kingdom life. If you cultivate this perspective, making decisions becomes part of the process of your personal growth and propels you into change.

Self-control to change.

Changing takes consistent effort as anyone who's tried to diet will know. I'm using dieting but any other example would do. In dieting, once you've decided to lose weight or some health issue is forcing a change in your eating, there must be a start point. **You have to be prepared to implement certain behaviours, foods, exercise, etc. and accept that, until further notice, this is what you're going to be doing. And immediately implement these.** That requires familiarising yourself with the kind of foods you'll eat, shopping for them, making sure you don't have wrong food stashes. Beyond the obvious, what else needs to change?

It also means you must have a clear vision of what you want to achieve. Self-control cannot work without a clear directive – you've got to frame what you want and know what it looks like. Set up a vision board with a picture of you at your ideal weight (be realistic). If you don't have such a picture, you can use a silhouette of someone of similar build to you. Now set out the feelings being at that ideal weight will bring. Set up pictures and statements on the vision board of what you will have once you reach your goal. Your brain works with pictures and by creating chemical snapshots filled with powerful emotion, your subconscious will see it as a real event and work with your brain to make it happen. I have written several books that explore various aspects of this, so feel free to resource them to help you. You will find them here.

https://www.amazon.com/author/rennieduplessis

If you're not sure how to start or what to do, please use my free 'Destiny Living Toolkit'. You can download the PDF here
https://thefluidway.com/wp-content/uploads/2020/08/Destiny-Living-Toolkit.pdf

Self-control to speak.

Psalm 19:14. "Let the words of my mouth and the meditations of my heart be acceptable in Your sight…" New science shows that positive words such as 'peace' and 'love' propel the motivational centres of the brain into action. Hostile language disrupts specific genes that play a key part in the neurochemicals that protect us from stress. A single negative word can increase the activity of our amygdala (fear centre of the brain), releasing stress producing hormones and neurotransmitters. In view of this, we understand why self-control in our speech is so important.

We use words to create because we are made in the image and likeness of God and when God speaks, things happen. David understood this and desires his mouth and his thoughts to be acceptable to God. **Whatever is in your inner world will pour out of your mouth (Matthew 12:34) and as a result, it will create substance in your life.**

Exercising the Fruit of self-control in this area enables you to create your life intelligently and in line with your God given destiny. **A good way to train yourself is by creating a Life Declaration for yourself and your loved ones.** Set out clearly what you would want in your life and add scriptures that confirm this. Spend time daily saying with intention out loud so you can hear it (you believe your own voice) and it can create. **Make sure your wording is in the present as if already done, because God functions in the present.** Mark 11:24.

Self-control to grow.

The Fruit is there to help you sustain a full, whole, happy life and self-control will empower you to sustain your growth. If you've followed through on the things we've covered, you're already growing – you just want to keep doing that. God is dynamic and as a kingdom dweller you're constantly going to face new challenges and new dimensions where you need to grow to flourish. It was the whole point of the Garden of Eden as we saw and God wants you to **use this ability to demonstrate through your life all the power and possibility of the kingdom of God.** More on this later in the book.

A word of caution…

Effective control.

Whenever we feel pressured that we have to do something, we run into motivational issues that will prevent long-term sustainability without burnout. If we feel that we 'have to' pray or whatever else, sooner or later that flesh-based enforcement will stop working and then we feel like failures and we're left miserable. How do we prevent this? Ephesians 5:1-21 Paul starts the chapter by stating we should walk in love, using Christ as our example of achieving this. He sets out a list of things to be avoided and finishes by giving these three keys to life in self-control:

-Changing our perception and perspective of ourselves. Ephesians 5:8-9 "…but now you are light in the Lord, walk as children of light: (for the fruit of the Spirit is in all goodness and righteousness and truth)." **Acknowledging and fully accepting who you are and what that means will change what's important to you.** Let me explain. If you're an Olympic athlete representing your country at the Games, you would behave in a certain way to best reflect what you represent. You would be courteous and compliant to rules without struggling to do so, simply because your focus is on the bigger picture. A lot of lack of control is based in selfishness and self-involvement. Cultivating the strong, kingdom mentality that you are a light bearer of that kingdom, diffusing the fragrance of Jesus, shifts your perspective. **This shift in perspective will move you from enforced morality (which never works) to decision-based living.** You don't do it because you have something larger and better that you want.

-Live aware of life. Ephesians 5:15-16 "See then that you walk circumspectly…redeeming the time." Walking circumspectly means to walk, looking around, by being aware of life around you. Why? So, you can redeem the time. In other words, invest your time in creating the life you want, living your destiny, "understanding what the will of the Lord is." **When you know where you're going in your life, you'll automatically and systematically cut out the things that hinder you in getting there.**

-Get 'plugged in' by being full of the Spirit. Ephesians 5:18-20 "…but be filled with the Spirit. Speaking to yourself in psalms, and hymns and spiritual songs, singing and making melody in your heart to the Lord. Giving thanks always…" **Spirit filled living releases the Fruit to live in gratitude**

and worship, freely fuelled by the juice of joy. It's in-the-zone empowered living.

The Gift of self-control harnesses and governs the power within in order to lead and to demonstrate a fragrant life without. So, for quick reference…

-Love is the fountainhead of everything, never failing and keeps on giving.

-Joy fuels our passion and is the juice of life.

-Peace gives wholeness in our mental realm to bring completion and sets us at one again.

-Longsuffering is mercy driven patience that teaches us how to relate in love in respect with people. Endurance (not a Fruit of the Spirit) is hope based in respect to things or circumstances for a desired outcome.

-Kindness makes us harmless, like a dove. It's the magnet that draws into love's effect. Kindness brings balance to the dynamic zeal for truth causing good in others which is found in Goodness.

-Faithfulness is the trusted steadfastness because we have character and integrity.

-Gentleness releases the real self in strength, truth and power.

-Self-control harnesses and governs the power within to lead and demonstrate a fragrant life without.

Will living like this make you happy? Let's explore what real happiness is and why God wants you to live a happy life…

WHAT DOES HAPPY LOOK LIKE?

**There is no key to happiness.
The door is always open.**

Isn't that a great statement? We're going to examine how you actually 'step through' the door and enjoy happiness. Looking beyond those shallow, breezy slogans that tell us "Happiness is something you switch on." and "Don't worry. Be happy!" Is happiness just adopting a glib saying? What makes us happy? Researchers collected and analysed findings from surveys on a global scale. In just one Gallup World Poll, 350,000 people from over 150 countries were surveyed. That's how seriously we treat the subject and how much energy we are spending to find the answer to happiness.

We all want to be happy and live happily and for all the knowledge out there on happiness, many people don't live happy lives. And yet it's achievable and sustainable beyond just being happy in the moment due to some good thing that happened in your life. **For the most part, I believe people don't achieve sustained happiness in their lives because they don't know what it looks like, don't know how to make it happen in their lives and don't treat it as a skill to develop.**

Our loving Creator made the most amazing and intricate synergistic system when He created us. Spirit, mind, and body perfectly blending into whole and happy living. **If that is true, we need to look at how happiness will impact us as a whole being, and what it will do to our wholeness if we live in a state of unhappiness.** Why should we bother working at being happy? Let's look at some physical benefits[8]:

1. Happiness protects your heart.

Research shows love and happiness are good for your physical heart. It predicts lower heart rate and blood pressure. Research[9] has also uncovered a link between happiness and heart rate variability, which refers to the time interval between heartbeats and is associated with risk for various diseases. Was happiness linked to healthier hearts among people with heart problems? Yes! Participants who rated themselves as happiest on the day their hearts were tested had a healthier pattern of heart rate variability on that day.

Researchers[10] invited people to talk about their anger and stress at work. They rated them on a scale of one to five for the extent to which they expressed positive emotions: joy, happiness, excitement, enthusiasm, and contentment. The researchers checked in 10 years later to see how the participants were doing. The happier ones were less likely to have developed coronary heart disease. In fact, for each one-point increase in positive emotions they had expressed, their heart disease risk was 22% lower.

2. Happiness strengthens your immune system.

Research[11] found a link between happiness and a stronger immune system. Investigating why happier people might be less susceptible to sickness[12], they gave volunteers the hepatitis B vaccine. After receiving the first two doses, participants rated themselves on nine positive emotions. The ones who were high in positive emotion were nearly twice as likely to have a high antibody response to the vaccine - a sign of a robust immune system. Instead of merely affecting symptoms, happiness works on a cellular level.

Another experiment[13] found that immune system activity in the same person goes up and down depending on their happiness. On days when they were happier, participants had a better immune response, as measured by the presence of an antibody in their saliva that defends against foreign substances.

3. Happiness combats stress.

Stress affects the brain and thinking and triggers biological changes in hormones and blood pressure. In the same study, researchers also found associations between happiness and stress. The happiest participants had 23% lower levels of the stress hormone cortisol than the least happy, and another indicator of stress - the level of a blood-clotting protein that increases after stress - was 12 times lower. Happiness also seems to carry benefits even when stress is inevitable. In the wake of inevitable stress, the hearts of the happiest participants recovered most quickly.

4. Happy people have fewer aches and pains.

A study[14] found that the health of the happiest participants improved over five weeks (and the health of the unhappiest participants declined). Positive emotion also mitigates pain in the context of disease. People who have positive emotion while dealing with chronic pain will recover faster and cope better with the pain.

5. Happiness combats disease and disability.

Happiness is associated with improvements in more

severe, long-term conditions as well, not just shorter-term aches and pains. In a study of participants who reported being happy and satisfied with life most or all of the time, they were about 1.5 times less likely to have long-term health conditions (like chronic pain and serious vision problems) two years later. Seniors can be afflicted by frailty, such as impaired strength, endurance, and balance and it puts them at risk of disability and death. In a study, people 65 and older rated how much self-esteem, hope, happiness, and enjoyment they felt over the past week. After seven years, the participants with more positive emotion ratings were less likely to be frail. Happier seniors were less likely to have a stroke in the subsequent six years; this was particularly true for men.

6. Happiness lengthens our lives.

In a famous study[15] of happiness and longevity, the life expectancy of Catholic nuns was linked to the positive emotion they expressed in an autobiographical essay they wrote upon entering their convent decades earlier. Researchers looked at these essays for expressions of feelings like amusement, contentment, gratitude, and love. In the end, the happiest nuns lived a whopping 7-10 years longer than the least happy.

Another study of adults ages 52-79 reported how happy, excited, and content they were multiple times in a single day. Here, the study found that the happier people were 35% less likely to die over the course of about five years than their unhappier counterparts.

In view of this small sample of evidence, it's clear that living in happiness enables our physical body to function better and live longer. As your body is the 'house' you live in while on earth that allows you to experience and live a whole, dynamic life, anything you can do to optimise and beautify your house should be included in your living regime. A merry heart truly does do good, and a broken spirit does dry the bones - it shrivels us up inside and narrows our lives. Proverbs 14:30a "A sound heart is life to the body" should read 'a healing or wholesome mind or inner self is life giving to the body' This scripture continues with envy (but it applies to any unchecked, negative emotion) rotting the bones, literally bringing decay to our essence or substance.

The other factors to happiness.

Scientists have determined that your happiness level is a result of a complex interaction of genes, behaviours, and life circumstances. While each person has a genetic set point for happiness (like we do for weight), a big chunk of how you feel is under your control (as with one's weight). Your mental wiring, your perspective on life, the way you relate and process life events and how you learn all factor into this. So, how you spend your time and the thoughts you allow to linger can really impact your mood and your long-term happiness. **Regardless of your happiness set point, you can live happy if you use the right tools, develop the skill and adjust your perspective.**

Research confirms that happiness involves developing our state of mind and resolving the factors that prevent us from doing that. Just saying or wishing you were happy won't make it happen. The good news is there are many things you can do daily to enhance your experience of bursts of happiness on a **consistent** basis. **Your life is made up of moments and what you do in every moment becomes the sum total of your life.** By filling your life with happy moments you will end up with happy years.

But what about dealing with long-term consistent happiness? Is it possible to be happy all the time in every day? To answer these questions we need to explore what the different types of happiness involve and what that looks like in your life. We'll look at these different types of happiness in the next few sections with ways for you to fold them into your life to make you happier. We are going to look at true happiness and how as a kingdom dweller armed and empowered by God you can live happily. It's a broad subject, so we'll look at the spiritual side as well as the mental and physical and see how you can implement immediate and long-term strategies. And while you explore this section I hope above all, that you'll have some fun with it.

We start the journey of happiness at the heart.

You're part of a joy-filled kingdom and your life is an expression of this kingdom. God empowered us to live and express this happy living when He created us. Proverbs 17:22 "A merry heart does good, like a medicine: but a broken spirit dries the bones" reads more closely that 'a merry heart effects a cure, literally, make well, sound or beautiful.' **That adds a whole dimension of empowerment to this scripture and reinforces why understanding and flowing in joyous living is vital to living a whole life.**

We know the bible meaning of the heart is the centre of you, your inner self, your control room of life. We call it mind. We've explored how you 'issue' your life from your heart (mind) and how everything, literally everything in your life starts from your heart. **The Spirit works through the heart with the Fruit to enable you to have a whole life. You cultivate the Fruit in your living and life and flow in Spirit empowerment to make that happen.** There's a great deal of co-operation that takes place between you using your mind and life and the Spirit, as we've already seen in this book. So, how do you 'work' your mind to make you happy?

Be real in your happy.

Factoring in who you are uniquely is very important. **The serious introvert is not going to express happy in the same way the bubbly extrovert will.** If you try and fashion your responses based on someone else you're going to make yourself very unhappy. By patterning your expression of happiness after someone else you're not responding in authenticity to yourself – **your genuine emotions and your responses are disconnected.** It's a form a masking, assuming a persona you think is acceptable to others or the way you should respond. (Patterning is a great tool if used correctly). To be effective you have to get comfortable in your own skin and understand how you uniquely experience happiness. So, the first step in the journey of happiness is understanding your own heart (mind).

We've looked at perspective, core beliefs and whole living and I've given you tools throughout the book to give you that understanding and implement change. We've systematically covered each area to bring you to this point where we can put our focus specifically on understanding happiness and strategies to live a happy life. **I'm going to give you real, quick ways to boost daily happiness levels and ways to develop happiness as a skill.** All this is going to happen in your inner world, so you'll have control over just how much happiness you live in and what form that happiness takes.

Even if you're habitually upbeat and happy your happiness will still be vulnerable and incomplete because you live in a physical dimension where many factors impact your life. How do your cultivate a merry heart in a world where there is injustice, pain, suffering? This is where your kingdom empowerment and perspective as a multi-dimensional being living a multi-dimensional life comes into play. By assuming what we have in the kingdom we live within that perspective, which in turn will determine our reality of the world. This is not pretending that everything is all fine but using our kingdom state of being in happiness that defines the quality of every moment of our lives. **In the open chest of the world, the contagion of your joy is a lifeline to a broken world.**

Remember the definition of Proverbs 17:22? 'A merry heart effects a cure.' **By living in a whole and happy state, within that kingdom perspective and empowerment you carry the power of heaven to the world.** You're not trying to 'fix' the whole world but you are creating a light-filled space in the world in which you can extend wholeness to others.

It's great that you can affect the world but how do you sustain happiness in yourself while you're doing it? How do you have a merry heart that effects a cure in your own life? **Achieving durable happiness requires two things: a change of perspective by you to realise happiness is a way of being and developing a skill to live like that. It requires sustained effort in training the mind and developing the Fruit to keep you in whole living.** Every section of this book has deliberately built the perspective of whole, joyous kingdom living and now it's time for us to focus specifically on maintaining a happy life.

Let's start with the basics of creating happy moments in your life that will add up to building a happy life...

Let's get Happy!

Your emotions in the moment have a profound impact on who you become.

The science of happiness shows that positive emotions are under our control far more than previously thought. Some people are just enduringly happy, that's just who they are. But what if that's not who you feel you are? What if you struggle with being happy? You may not have a naturally cheery outlook, but a positive one can be built through voluntary activities. This section is going to deal with how to habitualise your happiness, so, whether you're happy or not, we're going to bring some more happy into your life. **You're not going to fake it, you're going to develop the mindset of happiness.**

Research shows that we can enhance our experience of happiness on a consistent basis by working on our mental, physical and environmental factors. So what can you do to enjoy life more?

Happiness and contentment.

A surprise finding on happiness was that the happiest people in the world aren't the richest people in the most pleasant conditions or the wealthiest countries necessarily. **A key factor to the happiness of people who are less well-off is contentment.** Amazingly, slum dwellers living in some of the most deprived conditions, were content and often more so than people living in affluence. Why so? Although they lacked plumbing and other material assets, they had close social interaction and care for one another and their perspective was from this wholesome relational circle.

Becoming content.

Contentment is the state of mind in which we're satisfied

with what we have. **It's attitude focused and so, it's in our power to choose to be content!** Cultivating contentment with what you've got will bring a great deal of joy while you develop your life-long happiness. **By assessing each place in your life and finding those great things in your life that give contentment even if there are things in your life that make you unhappy, will keep you going.** Paul said, "I have learned in whatever state I am, to be content..." His life purpose was so fulfilling that he was able to treat hardships with a healthy perspective. **Regardless of conditions we can choose to be primed for happiness with the right perspective.**

Attitude Enhancers.

Be grateful for at least one thing every day, feel gratitude when you say it out loud. Be grateful to others and show them. A simple heartfelt 'thank you' is a two way blessing. Count your blessings, practise optimism about your future by looking at what you're building in your life, focus on good things, and avoid over analysis.

And action!

Are you prone to getting stuck in a funk? Here are some simple fun things you can do that will help you rewire your thinking:

-Put on some dance music, crank up the volume and dance! By focusing on and energizing your body, you will immediately feel the improvement in your mood. Does that sound simplistic? Researchers at the University of California Berkeley's Greater Good Science Center state that dancing causes the release of chemicals that are good for your brain: dopamine, oxytocin, serotonin, and endorphins. Here are some more effective ways to boost mood:

-Attend a lecture

-Go to an art gallery.

-Go to the theatre and watch a great performance.

-Take a long, luxurious bath and just soak and relax.

-Read an inspiring book or watch a funny movie.

-Cook a gourmet dinner for yourself or invite someone to cook with you and share the meal.

-Plant something and nurture it.

And laugh, laugh lots.

A merry heart does you good, it effects a cure in you and others - it's a proven fact.

So, enjoy life.

Looking at your photos, eating one of your favourite chocolates, enjoying a coffee with a friend, sitting in your favourite spot in the garden... **Consciously make time to practise these favourite little actions that we all have that give an instant shot of happiness and put a smile on your face.** These are very ordinary and very inexpensive but they create a flow of happiness. Create an environment for yourself that increases your happiness, treat yourself and others kindly and enjoy and express gratitude for who you are right now and where you are. Yes, it does take effort but you'll be so happy with the results.

Consciously make space in your day to do one of these favourite little actions and really sit in the moment to fully enjoy that favourite thing fully. Leave everything behind for those few moments and just enjoy! It's a mini holiday for your brain, it enhances your mood and it's giving you the opportunity to live in the moment. **Focus on enjoying little things, there are more of these in a day, and get into the habit of savouring life's pleasures and living in the moment.** Don't just watch that sunset, feel the breeze, listen to the sounds, feel how the air and atmosphere changes with the onset of night, stretch out your awareness and breathe. Relax. Be in the moment.

Little treats, big rewards

We need to be able to reward ourselves. Going out for dinner was identified as a factor that increased happiness. Just eating some chocolate was identified as high on the things that people said made them happy. I'm giving examples, you know what works for you specifically and what's good for your mental and physical health. By filling your life with little rewards, you create a happy flow that fills your life - happy moments that flow into a happy life. **As you get into the habit of doing this you can start using happy rewards for completing or achieving something.** For example, plan a weekend get-away with your partner or friend once you've completed that all-consuming difficult or draining task and just enjoy it. Leave your phone off, and get into your weekend get-away by doing lots of fun things together.

It's in the little details.

Be aware and take note - what things regularly make you happy, less happy? **Grow in your awareness of this and start replacing the unhappy things with happier things.** It sound like a no-brainer but invest your time in activities that make you happy. **Do more of what makes you happy and less of what doesn't.** Awareness of this will help you think about your happiness and help you let go of things that stand in the way. By appreciating the little pleasures in our everyday lives we can seriously boost our happiness.

In your happiness, you are the key player. No-one, not even God, can make you happy. God gave you free will, an amazing mind and a kingdom filled with gifts. What I want you to realise is just how much control you have over your happiness, so here we are going to deal with things you can and should invest your time in now to increase your level of happiness.

Let's start with one of my favourites that is fun and easy.

Your life is made up of moments, and what you do with the moments makes your life.

The research into neuro linguistic programming shows that some feelings can be induced without thoughts. By simply squaring your shoulders, lifting your chin, smiling with your mouth and your eyes and breathing in a slow manner while thinking of your favourite place in the world for 5 minutes (really be there), your mood will lift and your brain will release endorphins into your body to make you happy. If you do this often enough you will create a new habit. **Instead of passively being in an unhappy moment you will build a new response as your default setting.**

Once you've consistently done this for several months and it's your habitual response to unhappy it becomes a natural response. It becomes a well-worn neural pathway in your brain. When you then start feeling unhappy, your new default setting kicks in, your body signals you should square your shoulders, lift your chin, smile and breathe and your brain responds with endorphins to lift your mood. You have just habitualised your happy. Just before you go to bed at night, repeat your NLP exercise and allow your mind to be bathed in happy. Now tuck into bed and go to sleep in that cloud of happy so your subconscious can create around that state. One of many small steps you can take to start thinking right and being happy while the changes happen.

Habitually happy.

As we're on the subject of building habits, let's look at how to do it happily. Habits are powerful in bringing about lasting change. **One of the biggest reasons new habits don't 'stick' occurs when we try to change too much at once.** That's why I started with the simple NLP exercise. It's easy to remember, quick to do, has immediate benefits you'll remember that will motivate you to do it again. **As you consistently gain benefit from doing this one thing, your motivation level goes up, you gain confidence in your ability to change something and you actively do something with your realisation, all while building your happy!**

Why not stop reading right now and try this and once you've had your endorphin boost, write a reminder post-it note to keep around to remind you to build your happy habit doing this many times a day. Set it up on your phone with a reminder, do everything to help yourself develop happiness. Start using the simple exercise I gave throughout the day. Do it when you feel unhappy or stressed or when you just have a down moment. **Invest the action in your life to reap a dividend of happiness. Every time you do this you're piling on good benefits to your body and brain that you'll begin to notice.**

Let's spend some time now in defining what makes you happy and getting you happy while you grow into the full picture of happiness. In our leadership training I would always ask for very specific and very clearly defined areas that the organisation or individuals wanted to deal with. I would ask them to spend time to really think about it and define it. I want a clear picture with emotions and results that will follow. **Emotions and thoughts have different neural pathways in the brain.** That's why it's important to have a clear idea of both because if you do, you can harness the power of both in growing your new habit.

You may really want to change something but you can't change what you don't know. Once we had a clear well-defined single area to work with I'd ask: 'Why is this a problem to you?' even if it's obvious because I want them to hear themselves frame the situation. **By knowing what's not working, how it's affecting them and how it makes them feel, they have a clear picture of what they want to change.**

In growing happiness, how would you answer that question? Be specific. **You have to understand the situation, the actions and the feelings related to your unhappiness.** Next, I'd ask, 'What are you going to do to make a change happen?' **Many of us fail to change the situation because we haven't turned it into something to actually do.** Armed with the knowledge you have, what specific action should you take right now? How can you make this action part of your daily life? What stopped you from doing this before? How will you ensure it doesn't stop you going forward? Even if you can't give great, definitive answers to these questions don't let that stop you. Just start doing what you have decided to do daily and keep refining your strategy of how you'll keep doing it.

Actions tell you how you're going to do something. To succeed you must know what actions you're going to take. Applying this to your goal to be happier: **Saying, 'I want to be happy' is not something your mind can deal with – it's a statement without substance.** What does 'happy' look and feel like to you? How would your life look and be like if you're happier? Get a real picture of that. What already shows happy in your life and what doesn't? **You're building a life-long benefit that will impact your life,**

your health, your relationships and everyone you relate to, so take the time, ask the questions of yourself. Get serious about being happy. If getting a clear picture of what happy is to you is difficult for you, use my free resource to get you started and to plan the actions you will take to make it happen.
https://thefluidway.com/wp-content/uploads/2020/08/Destiny-Living-Toolkit.pdf

The 'bigger than' trigger.

At times, the good intention of an action just fizzles out and that new happier habit is never fully realised. **Here is my secret to success in dealing with this: Make sure the reason you are creating the new habit for is more important to you than what you've been doing because it's conviction (pure belief) that will propel you.** I knew a highly skilled Christian teacher who had taken up the habit of smoking even though she had severe lung issues. She seemed unable to stop even though it made her miserable. Then she was offered a prestigious post in a non-profit organisation and an opportunity of immigration to the USA. There was just one snag: the organisation had a declaration signed by all their workers that clearly stated you had to be tobacco and smoking free as they dealt with many addictive personalities. **To her, that was the 'bigger than' trigger.** She tossed out her cigarettes, signed the document and joined the organisation. Every time she felt a craving she'd simply say: 'I want this more than I want to smoke and it's much 'bigger than' a fleeting craving.' She spent a moment seeing what she's gained in her new post, felt her excitement and happiness, visualised her lungs clear, took a few deep breaths and immediately got up and did something constructive. She's never looked back.

By having a slogan - 'I want this more than I want to

smoke and it's much 'bigger than' a fleeting craving.' she reminded herself exactly why she was doing this and her belief kicked in and moved her forward. It was so successful because she followed her convicted slogan with feeling, visualisation and action. **Take a moment to set your 'bigger than' convicted slogan and the emotions and visualisation (your happy snapshot) that goes with it.** Really get a clear sense of how it feels because you want this to be a highly emotive brain chemical snapshot you can call up clearly and easily when you need it. Make your convicted slogan catchy and fun so your brain can play with it and you'll enjoy doing it.

Thoughts on gaining happy momentum.

Keep your happy momentum by looking back not forward. **That may sound counter-intuitive but looking at how far you've come in your life and the areas of your life that are filled with contentment and happiness will keep you going and will create encouragement and builds determination.**

Accept the stage of life that you're in right now and enjoy it. All the things that make you uniquely who you are are a result of your past and your current life. **Happiness can only be experienced in the present, so be here now.** Don't live in yesterday or tomorrow. Use what you have learnt throughout this book and the knowledge you already have and enjoy this moment. This is your life.

There are always good parts to even the hardest days. Find the good things in your life that are consistent and spend some time just being really, really grateful in yourself. Say it out loud so you can hear your own voice (because you believe your own voice) 'I'm so very grateful for...' Do it now before reading any further. Now, become aware how this simple act has changed the way you feel right now.

Some days it's just easier than others to hold onto what you are changing and keep going. Because your new behaviour is not yet a fully formed habit, you are guaranteed to mess up and slump back into old thinking patterns from time to time. **When you do, stop, say 'no, this is not where I want to be', use your habit changer slogan. Now do the NLP exercise and once you've finished immediately go and do something – don't sit around waiting to see if it really worked.**

As research has shown that 10% of our unhappiness is due to conditions in our lives, look at these and change them. Unhappy because you live in a cramped apartment? Declutter and organise better and think of clever ways to make your space happy, functional and pleasant. Try some colour, plants, textures and fabrics. Better still, have fun and play a little by creating your own wall art or some other unique stamp of yourself. It'll change the way you look at your apartment, give you something fun to do and make you happy. It's just about finding solutions to what makes you unhappy and your actions will lead to happier living.

Is there more? Yes

People who pray and feel connected spiritually were found to show greater contentment. By having a well-defined kingdom perspective, you walk in the knowledge of what a loving God has given you and how that has changed your life. You know the security of God's love and the empowering of the Holy Spirit and that increases your hope for the future and this affects your behaviour. While in prayer, spend some time talking to God about how you can make your life happier and thank Him that you are part of a joyous kingdom. Ask Him how you can take on more happiness and spread it around to others. Listen to what He says and then go and do it.

The happiest people have found the gifts and talents placed in them and are using them. Take a few online assessments to discover your strengths and weaknesses and how you can use both to grow. If you're not sure about your role in the kingdom, here is our free resource you can use to help you along.
https://thefluidway.com/wp-content/uploads/2020/08/My-Spiritual-Gifts-Profile-1.pdf

Take time to develop what you're good at and stretch yourself in new directions. It stretches you mentally and emboldens you to keep growing. Take on some creative project where you will need to develop new skills and have fun with it. You don't have to be a Picasso to enjoy painting or sculpting. **Do some things just for the pure joy of getting your hands dirty and be a kid again in creating.** If you take that attitude you won't go into a new activity looking to be perfect in it, you go in looking to do something happily. A playful attitude is great for your creative brain and your physical health.

Easy happiness keys to cultivate.

•Emotional health

-Be kind to yourself - you, like everyone have made mistakes, let go, it's past, so love yourself, enjoy your life and move on.

-Like you, everyone makes mistakes, so be tolerant of others.

-Allow yourself to be angry when appropriate but don't allow it to drown out your happiness. Seek to forgive everyone.

-Let go of negative emotions like resentment, bitterness, envy and actively think on wholesome emotions.

-Affirm yourself and others. It's healthy to compliment someone and it's healthy to receive genuine compliments.

Don't allow false modesty to rob you.

-Accept that life's good even if it's not perfect.

-Allow yourself to work through grief and loss. Sadness is useful. It's good to be sad 10% of the time when that's appropriate and it can be a time where you learn a great deal about yourself and life.

-Focus on good things not unpleasant things.

-Visualise good things. Start a vision board so you have something to put in front of your eyes that will lift you up and give your subconscious something to create.

-Smile and maintain good body language – it unconsciously boosts mood effortlessly.

•**Meaning in Life**

-Be generous. Both gratitude and giving bring happiness.

-Practise acts of kindness. Take the idea of a secret Santa into daily life and plan kind acts, kind actions and kind gifts.

-Help others and make a positive difference. Use everything you have to change the world around you. When you can, promote others and help them to their full life.

-Accept the difference you make even if it's small. Enjoy the sense of satisfaction and be happy in the difference you make by acknowledging it to yourself.

-Make the world around you a better place. Bless your neighbourhood with a daily blessing, volunteer, do something that changes things around you.

-Be active in changing policies - it's empowering. Use your voice and abilities to help those who aren't empowered to help themselves.

•Caring relationships

-Nourish a loving, quality, long-term relationship. Stop and enjoy what you have, show and express appreciation, love and support. Make time to appreciate and grow in intimacy.

-Surround yourself with people who look out for you, people who care and who you care for in return.

-Cultivate a few quality, close friends (happiness doesn't increase with the number of friends). Spend time and relate.

-Focus on people who look out for you, encourage you and don't harm you or others. Do the same for them and tell them how much they mean to you.

-Encourage, love and care for those in your life. Purposely cultivate awareness of them and their lives. Hug them often and tell them you love them and then follow that up by expressing it in your actions.

•Healthy living

-Activity in work and recreation boosts happiness. Being active for fun or purpose is good for your body and brain, helps you relate and interact and builds your life.

-Get some sunlight to boost mood or just go outdoors. Look around, enjoy the feel of the wind, the light on the leaves, the smells and sounds. By doing so, you've brought yourself into the present so your brain can get creative. It also makes you appreciate where you are. Happy!

-Exercise, brisk walking can raise mood levels. Get out into nature and just enjoy the act of moving in a nice environment.

-Remove habitat toxins such as nerve and behaviour deteriorating chemicals found in foods, household products, water and air. Eat pure, organic foods, check ingredients in foods, cosmetic and household products and do a house detox.

-Check the side effects of your medications especially look for depression side effects. Ask your physician for safer alternatives, if possible. If not, use one of the other suggestions here to lift your mood.

-Eat foods that nourish and enhance well-being and mood. Note the short and long term mood changes from what you consume and stop eating those foods that depress you.

-Boost nutrition with minerals, vitamins and nutrients that reduce irritability, depression. Get the right medical and supplemental advice tailored to your physiology to boost happiness. Get your health care professional to advise you.

-Reduce distress by reducing over commitment. If you're struggling with this, re-read the Fruit of self-control and consider your schedule priorities carefully. Remember, a happy, whole life is not achieved by cramming it full but by living fully aware in every moment.

-Maintain enough deep sleep and relaxation time. This includes fun time with family and friends and some alone time for just you.

•Work satisfaction

-Find work that gives you satisfaction, that's meaningful for you, where you're appreciated. If that's not possible, find a hobby or a church activity that will give satisfaction and where you will be appreciated.

-Reduce your time commuting to work. An hour's journey to

work significantly reduces happiness. Non-commuters are happiest. Higher earnings don't compensate for the time lost as time is your most priceless commodity.

-Develop expertise in some things you enjoy e.g. your art, writing, advising, decorating, research etc. whatever works for you personally. Take time to do these things and enjoy it when you're doing it.

Body hacks that make you happy.

Your body and brain work in concert and these are great ways to use your body and your brain to make you happier instantly.

1. Walk the happy walk. Scientists at Canada's Institute for Advanced Research[16] had two groups of study participants walk on a treadmill, one with their shoulders slumped and with a slow gait, and the other in a more cheerful fashion. As they walked, the test subjects were shown a list of positive and negative words. The depressed walkers remembered more negative words, while the cheerful walkers remembered the upbeat words on the list, so their body language during the test had affected their moods and memory. The lesson here? Lift your head, extend your gait, it will signal your brain and change the way you view things.

2. Smile. You know the saying 'Fake it until you make it'? Well, it's actually true when it comes to smiling[17]. Research has shown that even a manipulated smile can boost your mood. A genuine smile - one that involves both the mouth and the eyes, releases endorphins into your bloodstream and boosts your immune system. A University of Kansas study found that people who smile[18] have better heart recovery rates after stressful events. So, if you find yourself in a stressful situation, use a smile to signal your body and brain to kick in some happy.

3.Power pose. Restore your confidence through striking a power pose[19]. Put your hands on your hips like Superman, spread your legs slightly and straighten your back and look straight ahead of you and then hold for a few moments. 'Power posing' can help reduce cortisol (stress hormone) levels while increasing feel-good hormones and makes you project better.

4.Laugh. The power of laughter as a mood booster is worth repeating. Laughter[20] allows your muscles to relax, improves blood sugar, and raises and then beneficially lowers blood pressure levels, according to the Mayo Clinic. Because laughing is often a social thing (you're 30% more likely to laugh with others than alone), it decreases isolation. Although your brain can detect the difference between real and fake laughter, sometimes starting off with a fake ha-ha will get you going to the real thing.

6.Spread your limbs and take up some space. When you're feeling nervous, uncertain or afraid, you may find yourself crossing your arms or legs, scrunching your body up or using your hands to cover your face or mouth. That's called 'body blocking', and it's a sign of discomfort. To feel better, spread out the space you fill, uncross arms and legs, straighten up and take up more space. Making yourself and your space bigger conveys confidence, not just to those around you, but also to your brain.

Be primed for happiness and walk in it. Invest in your happiness by incorporating these things and see your happiness soar. Now that you have happy days, we can turn our attention to building the skill for enduring happy living.

Growing Happiness

"Now and then it's good to pause in our pursuit of happiness and just be happy." Guillaume Apollinaire

Armed with an arsenal of simple things you can do to create your happy moments that build into a happy life, we are able to enjoy happiness now and we are equipped to sustain happiness beyond the happy moments of life. What skill should you cultivate to build a happy life?

I mentioned earlier that I believe that people don't achieve sustained happiness in their lives because they don't know what it looks like, don't know how to make it happen in their lives and don't treat it as a skill to develop. We've identified what happiness looks and feels like to you through your considered questions and how to create happiness daily through simple, easy do-able actions that form new happiness and thinking. As happiness is a skill, a manner of being, we're now ready to look at developing the skill.

A skill is the ability to do something very well, and as with everything in life, you're good at something because you've learnt how to do it well. Happiness is no different. **It's developing the mindset that happiness is a state of being – it's your foundation and your default setting, the sane and profound way of living and thinking.** Accepting that as your life perspective will aid you in tailoring your learning and growing to maintain and enlarge your perspective of living this way.

Learning to be.

So, from your earlier considered questions, how do you learn best? Do you like reading words, demonstrations, visuals, stories or listening to things being explained? Think back on what you did in the past that helped you learn something well. What made learning difficult? How would you use your way of learning to develop the skill of being happy?

Whichever blend of learning styles that works best for you, apply it in what we'll cover in this section. And remember, one of the quickest ways to learn something new, and practise it is to teach others how to do it. Share what you've learnt even if you feel you don't know everything, it keeps your learning focused and practical and will help you to keep developing your skills. As you learn, take time to think about what you're learning. How has it changed you? Being excited about the change your learning is bringing (big or small) is a great motivator to keep you growing the skill of being happy. And keep doing the happy things you discovered in the last section while you're developing your skill of being.

Remember, it takes about six months to fully develop a new skill and all of what is happening inside you may not be fully evident to everyone around you. Don't let that put you off and just enjoy your happy daily routine and build your happiness state. Just keep building your skill of being happy and spend time with happy people, it does 'rub off'.

Using cell memory to build the state of being happy.

We looked at habitualising happiness earlier and this plays into developing the skill, because once it's a habit it becomes almost automatic. Take, for example, playing the piano. Once you have memorized the music through hours of practice, your fingers will automatically play the piece. Your brain has created well-worn neural pathways through the repetitive action of practice. **This is an example of muscle memory working with mind potential and brain learning to produce a result.** Memory operates in the whole body, on a cellular level. Think of the last time you drove your car all the way home through traffic, performing complex decisions and manual dexterity without conscious thinking! We do it all the time without realizing it.

Once learned, responses become almost automatic. Your changed responses and thoughts in your inner world work out through your heart and 'issues' your life. The more automatic your new happy thinking becomes, the easier it is to maintain the new happy thinking, the stronger the effect on your body and life and so on... **It's a cycle of growth that has gained momentum through previous change that now makes future growth in happiness easier.**

Mindset change to build your skill of being.

While looking at the way you learn, you would have encountered some self-talk you attach to your learning that isn't helpful. In understanding your mental wiring, your way of thinking and identifying any mindsets that could get in the way of your life, you can get the right mindset to move you on. Learning leads to doing and your goal is a state of being happy. You also want to have the right mindset as foundation when you use intention to create in your life (more in the next section). You want to 'clear out' any negative mindsets that could get in the way of this. Let's look at this.

-Do you find it hard to see the world in anything but shades of grey or do you think the future is gloomy and you're fixed in who you are in a world where everyone else is doing better than you? The best cure to this is proving yourself wrong and the best way to do that is by finding something that you're passionate about and doing it with all your heart without looking to the outcome. Don't judge it or compare it, just do it. Use your 'bigger than' slogan and visualisation to help you along just as we saw in the last section.

-Do you fear losing control or think things are far worse than they are, and do you underestimate your ability to be able to face the consequences or challenges in your life? Do you avoid acting because you feel you're ill equipped? The best cure for this is to take a self-inventory of your successes and strengths. The fact that you have navigated life successfully up to this point shows you have latent abilities - be proud of that. Find safe ways to express and frame your fears and really look at them. Ask, 'Is this true of this situation?' and 'What is the evidence of that?' In view of what you've learnt in this book, how can you personally change the way you think? How will you do that?

-Do you find it hard to learn from others and believe you really know more and have superior abilities to everyone else? Are you finding it hard to build relationships because of how you view others and do you have bouts of depression? The best cure for this is to consciously appreciate the efforts of those who you interact with. Consciously approach each day with a belief that you're going to meet amazing people that you'll learn from and find opportunities that will teach new things to you.

-Do you believe you can't change, that your behaviour is fixed and that means you will always act and do things the same way? Do you like doing things in the same way and do you refuse to try other ways? The best way to deal with these is by acknowledging that God is dynamic, we live in a dynamic kingdom and we can't do that by staying the same. Remember, there's no such thing as failure, just unacceptable outcomes. Start small by changing one area in your life that will take you out of your comfort zone and grow a new skill.

Finding what mindset you're defaulting to and changing your thought life will help you build a mindset of growth - the foundation we want to develop to build our skill to bring us to a joyous state of being, with your inner world flowing out and growing your happiness.

Picking apart the skill of being happy.

Like a really good stew that has many ingredients to create the perfect blend of flavours, a skill is made up of different ingredients. Let's look at those ingredients. We want to keep this fun, so I'm going to recommend you look at https://www.happify.com/ because they have great visual aids and fun exercises to increase your happiness. They base their programs on the basis of five key happiness skills:

Savouring[21] "is the practice of noticing the good stuff around you, taking the extra time to prolong and intensify your enjoyment of the moment, making a pleasurable experience last for as long as possible - the idea is to linger, take it in, and enjoy the experience. Eventually it'll become a habit - one you'll never want to break. Those who regularly and frequently savour are happier, more optimistic and more satisfied with life." You can take this even further by remembering and savouring happy past things through reminiscing, savour future things through positive anticipation and savour present things by being present in the moment.

Thank[22] is "the act of identifying and then appreciating the things people do for us. It fills us with optimism and self-confidence, knowing that others are there for us. It dampens our desires for 'more' of everything - and it deepens our relationships with loved ones. And when we express our gratitude to someone, we get kindness and gratitude in return. The practice of gratitude can increase happiness levels by around 25%, it's not hard to achieve and cultivating gratitude brings other health effects, such as longer and better quality sleep time."

Aspire[23] is "feeling hopeful, having a sense of purpose, being optimistic. Studies show people who have created meaning in their lives are happier and more satisfied with their lives. Genuine optimism is a friend magnet. It also makes your goals seem attainable and your challenges easier to overcome. Bottom line: you'll not only feel more successful, you'll be more successful. A person's level of hope is shown to correlate with how well they perform tasks. Using one's strengths in daily life, studies have found, curbs stress and increases self-esteem and vitality. Believing that your goals are within reach promotes a sense of meaning and purpose in life - a key ingredient of happiness."

Give[24] "When you give someone something, you make them happier. The giver, not the receiver, reaps even more benefits. Being kind makes us feel less stressed, isolated and angry, and it makes us feel considerably happier, more connected with the world, and more open to new experiences." Purpose to do six random acts of kindness a week and plan them beforehand. It will immediately lift your mood and increase your happiness. It will also change your thinking positively.

Empathise[25] is "the ability to care about others. It's the ability to imagine and understand the thoughts, behaviours or ideas of others, including those different from ourselves. When we empathise with people, we become less judgmental, less frustrated, angry or disappointed - and we develop patience. We also solidify the bonds with those closest to us. And when we really listen to the points of view of others, they're very likely to listen to ours. Strong relationships are essential to happiness, and practising empathy will nurture the relationships in your life." Compassion is a skill that we can all learn.

Did you notice that every skill mentioned in growing

in happiness is incorporated in kingdom living?

Let's look at that. Our kingdom perspective allows us to enjoy and savour living; the magnitude of what we've been given brings joy and makes us thankful; and by knowing the empowerment we have, we can aspire to develop our life to the full; which makes us want to give of ourselves and the bounty we have in the kingdom to others; because we empathise and care for others. It's all there in our kingdom life. All we have to do is develop what's been given to us, and for that, we have our minds and the Fruit working together to make it happen.

Suffering and happiness.

It's great to grow in happiness when we're just living in the normal flow of life, and, apart from normal ups and downs, everything is going well. But what if it's not? You live in a physical dimension where many factors impact your life. How do your cultivate a state of happiness in a world where there is injustice, pain, suffering?

In the hard things that my partner and I endured, we used this: 'If you're going through something difficult, keep going.' It's sounds simplistic, but it's a healthy perspective. By mentally acknowledging that things change (that this too shall pass), that God is dynamic and your life is fluid and changing, you'll find the encouragement to not stop in the pain and so lose the momentum of your life.

If it's an illness or something with external circumstances you have little control over, this statement can be hard because you can't change things. **You can change how you live through an unchangeable situation. Purposely invest a part of your day no matter how small into doing happy things beyond this illness or circumstance.** For example, if you're fatigued from long-term-illness, take time as you rest to think creatively of what you want to do when you are well or, if its lifelong, what you want to build. **Make your life, right now, about more than what you're going through.**

Use the key skills to happiness we covered earlier in this section and develop them in your life. Focus on the things that bring contentment in your life and also, like Paul, operate in your life purpose - it will enable you to treat hardships with a healthy perspective. For example, if you're a great teacher but you're bedridden, record your teachings and get someone to type and format them into a book you can publish and bless the world with. Find a way to enlarge your life and the lives of those around you in a manner that will bring joy.

Use the Fruit to empower you during your times of hardship or suffering. **Never look to suffer but if you are in a hard place, find out why you are there and what you can learn from it.** Re-look at desert places in the section headed 'In for the long haul' and spend time to strengthen your endurance through following the points we covered there.

Both frustration and fatigue can rob us of our state of being and if you find this to be true, this is time to stop and frame that frustration. You have tools to deal with this – keep going even if it's slow and nothing seems to be happening, you are growing, your Fruit is growing, your kingdom life is growing. If you're just tired of being tired, bone weary of the struggles or sickness, know that you're never alone. Wrap yourself in the safety of God's loving arms and rest there awhile. Spend time doing your NLP exercise, it rejuvenates. Make a point even in your tiredness to exercise building your happiness skills.

True happiness for you, as a multi-dimensional being, can only be found in the life lived in a kingdom perspective in the flow of the Fruit of the Spirit. We live and move and have our being in God – it's our state of being that has the **potential** of lasting happiness, realised by our mental effort to make it so. Keep the kingdom perspective and make the choices of how you want your kingdom living to unfold. Build your happiness skills and form life-changing habits by taking what you have read in this book and transforming it into action. Optimism, kingdom confidence, gratitude, hope, compassion, purpose, empathy - these are all qualities that anyone can own. You just have to learn how by acting on what you know.

All the dynamic creativity, power and healing of the Fruit is evident in your life and that makes you different in the best possible way. You are transforming those around you by enhancing their lives. You act differently and respond differently. Those around you sit up and take notice. And this isn't just in your circle of friends, your boss, your children or spouse – you can change the world around you through the power of intention. By doing this, you operate just like God.

Armed with this knowledge, we can now turn our attention to intentionally creating the life you want…

THE ART OF CREATIVE LIVING

"…now you are light in the Lord. Walk as children of light. For the fruit of the Spirit is in all goodness, righteousness and truth." Ephesians 5:8-9

All of whole and happy living is contained in these few words! A trustworthy roadmap, one based on cultivating the conditions for genuine well-being. Note the scripture declares that you are light. You're radiating the light and love of God all the time when you walk in the fullness of what we've covered in this book. **Whole and happy living carries with it an influencing field – it's contagious in the best possible way.** When we 'rub off' wholeness and happiness we are in fact revealing to the world the power of a Fruit filled Spirit led life. This was God's intention for our lives and guided His considered thought and action in creation.

This is how God's thinking works. What He thinks comes into being.

Hebrews 11:3 "By faith we understand that the worlds were framed by the word of God, so that the things which are seen were not made of things which are visible." God has a way of creating new things that are completely different out of nothing that is tangible or available. In other words, **He** uses the non-existent to manifest the existent! Revelation 4:11b "...You created all things, and by Your will they exist and were created." God thought about something new that He was about to create out of nothing. **He thought it out and created it and used His will to continue the existence of that creation.** We understand this because we ourselves use the image and likeness of God in ourselves to speak creatively and create tangibly.

We create by thinking, then by doing just like God.

We all have an influencing field that extends beyond ourselves and our lives and impacts those around us and the world. **Your thoughts, working into your life, create in your life and the lives of those around you.** Your thoughts and how you think are coloured by, and interconnected to, your inner world. We produce our treasure or life from the inside out, not the outside in.

No thought we have is created or emanates as an individual or unique and freestanding thing or event. Think of a lemon. See it in your hand as you slowly peel off the skin and the oily, citrus smell is released and diffuses into the air. There's a waxy feel of its skin on your fingers as you peel it back to reveal the pulp inside. Take a segment and sink your teeth into it and feel the pulp pop and release the tartness of the juice into your mouth and run over your tongue. Slowly chew the pulp and feel the tightening sensation along your jaw... See what I mean? Most people at this point will have a strong salivary gland response to the thought that manifests as if the lemon eating were really happening right now. **Our minds treat our thoughts as real and tangible and bring bodily and mental responses to the reality of this place and moment in time. Thinking produces real time responses and realities.** The lemon we ate before produces a reality in real time even in the absence of a real lemon in the now. We've just used the 'lemon memory' to determine a reality and a body memory response to that reality in this moment.

Your mind is the most powerful tool you possess. It connects the physical to the spiritual and determines how you live. The Israelites accepted a physical deliverance from the bondage of slavery but remained slaves mentally. The crucible in which our tomorrow is forged contains the thoughts and intents of our mind today. We won't think or live beyond the borders our inner world frames around our lives. Proverbs 23:7a "For as he thinks in his heart, so is he."

Every thought is moving towards some ultimate creation. Because you were made in the image and likeness of God, you have the need to expand and enlarge yourself and your life. You want to harness that constantly creating power of the mind to build your life of purpose.

John 15:16 "You did not choose Me, but I chose you and appointed you that you should go and bear fruit, and that your fruit should remain, that whatever you ask the Father in My name He may give you." **Christ wants your life to be fruitful in every dimension, not just spiritually.** In your journey of living in the full potential of what your mind is capable of, you must take the step beyond renewal to intentioned living. What do I mean by this? **You have to recognize that you have the ability to create and that you are creating every day.** And just like a scientist in a laboratory carefully mixes the ingredients and follows the laws that govern the ingredients he is working with, we too, must adopt an attitude of awareness into what we are creating.

The gift of intention.

God built into us the ability to create just like He does

because we have His image and likeness in us. Hebrews 2:6b-8 tells us that we have been crowned with glory and honour and "set (humans) over the works of Your hand." So God has given us as kingdom dwellers the ability to access anything that God made – it's available to us through intention and action. It's out of the abundance of our inner life that we produce our living and relating. Luke 6:45 "A good man out of the good treasure of his heart, brings forth that which is good... for out of the abundance of his heart his mouth speaks." Your heart is the centre of you, the control room of your life. Through your God-given free will you are in charge of what you allow into your inner world, how you process what is there and what that produces in your life. You got the light, but you must let it shine and produce 'of the light'. **This is not just being a spiritual light, you are light in every part of your life and living.**

There's no doubt about the power you have through kingdom living. All of eternal heaven and all of what God released through Jesus is yours. Living in touch with this flow of heaven's power and possibility is what gives you the opportunity to create a life of purpose and destiny. Jesus lived it and He taught it because He expects us to live fully as multi-dimensional beings in a multi-dimensional life. When we do, we are living advertisements for the kingdom.

Create like Jesus from a kingdom perspective.

Luke 9:54-56 "And when His disciples James and John saw this, they said, 'Lord, do you want us to command fire to come down from heaven and consume them, just as Elijah did?' But He turned and rebuked them, and said, 'You do not know what manner of spirit you are of. For the Son of Man did not come to destroy men's lives but to save them.'"

Jesus "rebukes" them because this is completely contrary to everything He has been teaching them about the kingdom.

He draws their attention to the spirit, the intent, they are operating in. He doesn't dispute that they have the ability to call down fire, and He doesn't dispute what Elijah did. He's focusing them on their heart intent and His true message of saving, not destroying. Why is this so important? **Jesus wants them to operate their empowerment and create an environment of life.** Jesus taught that as a man thinks in his heart, so is he. That heart power is working through you every day, with every thought you think, you are creating. Your heart is 'issuing' your life as Proverbs 4:23 states. In order to create the optimum environment of growth, we use the mind to intentionally create the 'issues', the flowing out, of our lives.

What is intention?

Intention is the thoughtful and considered action you put to your desire and includes a clear vision, a desire and action. The law of reciprocity works - what you sow you reap. Thoughts become things and you can make the process more effective by understanding and operating in intention correctly.

Intention flows with emotion, mental snapshots, thoughts, words, all creating as it flows. If these, like those of the disciples in the above scripture are charged with hatred, anger, revenge, jealousy and other negative harmful emotions, that flow is working both ways. **Intention works both ways, as you're creating you're influencing your creation and being influenced by that creation.**

Pure intention.

Ephesians 3:20 "Now to Him who is able to do exceedingly abundantly above all that we ask or think, according to the power that works in us." **This is Godly power in us at our disposal that works through and**

above our thinking and asking.

I was appalled in an election at how many people were using prayer and intention to influence an election with a 'win at any cost' attitude – even if that meant undermining the democratic process, the laws of the country and the rights of those who voted differently. Don't misunderstand me, I believe prayer is integral to civic life and we should intention and use our civic power to change things. But we should copy God in how we go about it and ask, what manner of spirit am I of? Luke 9:54-56. **What am I channelling into and what am I channelling through my life with this intention?** Luke 6:45.

Pure speech, not spells.

The bible refers to witchcraft (incanting certain spells to influence or affect the outcome at another's expense) as something kingdom believers should avoid. We know these work as we see when Moses faces Jannes and Jambres in Pharaoh's court. Exodus 7 – 9. Intent, words and actions create.

To understand just how dangerous and destructive it is to put intention and desire to something in the wrong spirit, I'm going to share a shocking, true story with you:

There was a family in South Carolina who loved litigation. The couple had a very clear sense that if they could sue someone they could get rich very quickly. The man told his friends that he and his wife believed that they'll get one million dollars by suing someone. (This was in 1992 when a million dollars was considered to be a lot of money for someone working at minimum wage). They would talk about it all the time and truly believed it. The end of the story is they did receive a million dollars in a settlement for their daughter who had a horrific accident and was tragically killed.

And they collected their million dollars, just as they'd put their faith out for. Their lives were destroyed and they never recovered emotionally. Desire driven intention without the Fruit-filled life and considered thought and action is not the way to use this ability we have.

Intent works on pure, creative power which should be used in thoughtful, considered ways, like Jesus. You can use your intent, in the Fruit of the Spirit to create wonderful blessings for yourself and those around you and in the world.

Steps to intentioned creative living.

If you've worked through the Toolkit you have a very clear idea of your life and you would have implemented some things that should already be bearing fruit in your life. If you haven't yet done so, please take a moment and print out My Destiny Living Toolkit© and then take some time to read through it. It will give you the steps on how to build your vision and the tools to create the life you want. https://thefluidway.com/wp-content/uploads/2020/08/Destiny-Living-Toolkit.pdf

The point about creating is that you do so in a considered manner. You think about what you want and how to achieve that and then do that. Your thoughts must be clear because they are seeds. They must be planted and cared for. You shouldn't over think them. Let the seed grow by loving and nurturing your vision and staying in the light. Know who you are and what you're capable of as a kingdom dweller and have steadfast belief that your seed will bear fruit.

"And the Lord answered me, and said, 'Write the vision, and make it plain upon tables, that he who reads it may run.'" Habakkuk 2:2. **Your written vision gives you the motivation and the direction to move forward.** Look at your vision board, spend time in your perfect day, let this be very real to you right now. You are using the 'lemon memory' principle we dealt with earlier and your body and brain will respond as if it's real.

Creative living in real time.

Living in the now is a completely creative state where you allow yourself to create or find and access whatever you need to propel a life of power. Wow! That's amazing. It comes down to awareness - knowing you have this ability and knowing what you're capable of, if you tap in and release it. **You remove the limits you've set for yourself that are false that you've accepted unquestioningly.** By changing your perspective from 'Can I do this?' to 'How can I do this?' you move the **situation away from the outcome into the process and this is where all the power of your mind finds expression.** You start creating!

We all know this scripture: "Therefore, I say unto you, whatsoever you desire, when you pray, believe that you have received, and you shall have them." Mark 11:24. Here is the original translation from the Aramaic: **"Ask without hidden motive and be surrounded by your answer. Be enveloped by what you desire that your gladness may be full."** Wow! Surround yourself with the reality of your answer, see it as real right now. Your vision, your intention, your thoughts, your actions flowing through a life lived in the Fruit creating what you want and you receiving it in gladness.

Be patient and live a Fruit-filled life while you create daily. As you receive a part or whole of what you're creating, write it down on your vision board under "I gratefully received it" and date it. Then spend time in gladness about it, it's the juice that will move you further.

You have risen to the challenge and incorporated the Fruit

in your life in a whole new level and you will continue to see the wholeness in your life and the lives of others as you live in this. The Spirit is working with you through your mind and life to make this happen. Our minds work in feedback loops we can actually use to our advantage. In creative living, once you have created the right inner world you can allow it to run so that continuous blessing of whole and happy living is your way of life. Enjoy your life!

One Last Thing...

If you enjoyed this book or found it useful, I'd be very grateful if you'd post a short review on Amazon.

https://www.amazon.co.uk/dp/B08MYXVDQ6

Your review will help other readers make an informed decision when buying books. Reviews and ratings also move the book up in Amazon ratings, so it's more easily found on Amazon and helps me reach new readers on Amazon.

Your support really does make a difference and I read all the reviews personally. I would also appreciate it if you would help me get the word out about my books by letting others know, particularly via Facebook, Twitter etc.

To find out when my next book is due for release, follow me on my Amazon page to get all the latest news.
https://www.amazon.com/author/rennieduplessis

Thanks again for your support!

ABOUT THE AUTHOR

To learn more about me or to follow me

https://www.amazon.com/author/rennieduplessis

Dr Rennie Du Plessis has earned two PhD degrees; one in Theology and Religion and another in Counselling Psychology. A highly experienced instructor in practical, applicable biblical principles with a vast range of expertise, Dr Du Plessis has taught internationally at all levels; from foundational instruction through to specialized instruction to senior leaders, from recovering addicts to doctorate students. Dr Du Plessis' books are based on more than forty years in continuous study, research, writing and instructing to learners at all levels.

A love of asking the hard questions and exploring truth has resulted in many profound and amazing discoveries which are reflected in this book. There is an authoritative depth and clarity that comes from this breadth of knowledge, understanding and expertise and most importantly, from decades of practical experience. Dr Du Plessis draws insights from personal explorations of Religious Practices, Theology, Cognitive and Competency Developing, Cognitive Counselling, Temperament Diagnostics, Anthropology, and History to name a few disciplines.

These books are for real people living in the real world. This practicality is a reflection of Dr Du Plessis' extensive business experience: entrepreneur, multiple business owner, author, trainer, radio announcer, cognitive counsellor and international speaker. It brings a practical, workable aspect to all the training and writing. Dr Du Plessis conducts workshops, seminars, lectures internationally and has developed and created courses on the wide scope of living a life of possibility.

Dr Du Plessis loves educating and inspiring others to succeed and to live the life of their dreams and says, "Making our world a better place and helping people and businesses develop is a way of life to me. I passionately believe that each life can make a difference to the world and I put great emphasis on the personal development of the whole person. The potential in us excites me and is the passion behind my forty years of people development. It's an amazing adventure giving someone the power of knowledge that flips the switch and watching as they realise all the possibility and power residing inside them." The books by Dr Rennie Du Plessis are the distilled essence of all this passionate knowledge made available to you.

OTHER BOOKS BY THE AUTHOR

We have new releases every few months, so follow us on Amazon

The Bridge of Possibility: How to link the physical and the spiritual to release your destiny

https://www.amazon.co.uk/dp/B07Z787J3H

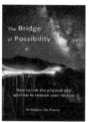

This book will explain how you can use the bridge of possibility to:

Understand and release the power within you.

Understand the staggering possibilities in you and partner with God by releasing your full creative abilities.

Understand the mind of Christ and release all latent power and potential available to you.

Understand your destiny and use the tools to achieve.

Thoughts on the Way

A selection of our reader's favourites. Short, powerful and concise teachings on Christian life and living.

Beautiful One: Jesus Revealed.

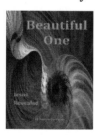

Journey through the bible in a full discovery of Jesus. Meet the Son, the Messiah, the Man as we unfold the greatest love story ever told

Prayer Power

Tales out of Africa: Ordinary People having Extraordinary Encounters with God.

GIFTS for DESTINY and LIFE
https://www.amazon.co.uk/dp/1838021000

The Fruit of the Spirit: the way to whole and happy living

The Little Book on Church Counselling
https://www.amazon.co.uk/dp/B07YGW8XNC
How can we meet the needs of hurting people in a church and bring them to

wholeness? What do we need to do to create a safe, wholesome environment with an effective counselling network? How can church counsellors develop effective skills, empathy and sensitivity to function in power? This book offers a model for a church to function in power. We will explore biblical principles, the mind and the tools to meet the needs of all. Benefit from sound, biblical and psychological best practice recommendations that will help you set up, develop and perfect your church counselling to heal the hurts and bind the wounds of all.

The Holy Spirit Book
https://www.amazon.co.uk/dp/B086N4PRBT
Discover who the Holy Spirit is, what He's like, what He does and why He was
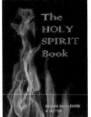
given to us.
Find out how to have a personal relationship with Him and how He'll help you.
Learn how to be empowered and gifted by the Holy Spirit and use these to transform your life and the lives of others.

Create your New Mind: Solve the Mind Puzzle and Create the Best Version of You
https://www.amazon.com/gp/product/B07Y5WC9GW
Would you like to better understand your mind and the incredible power God
placed in it?
Starting from the foundation of the bible, this comprehensive book will show:
-how the mind works and how you can operate in a mind without limits and the possibilities released in your life.
-how to program your subconscious to let go of blocks preventing you from moving forward.
-clear, easy steps to living a life of destiny with tools to help
others to a powerful life.

REFERENCES AND CITATIONS

Website information is correct at the time of publishing. However, no liability can be accepted for any information or links found on third-party websites which are subject to change.

https://thefluidway.com/wp-content/uploads/2020/08/Destiny-Living-Toolkit.pdf

https://thefluidway.com/wp-content/uploads/2020/08/My-Spiritual-Gifts-Profile-1.pdf

https://www.happify.com/

Cover image Pixabay CC0

https://pixabay.com/illustrations/smiley-emoji-emote-symbol-emoticon-1041796/

Books and references.

1.'The Holy Spirit Book' Rennie Du Plessis and A Victor
https://www.amazon.co.uk/dp/1999720555

2.'Create Space' Derek Draper
https://www.amazon.co.uk/Create-Space-Manage-Productivity-Success

3.'The Bridge of Possibility: How to link the physical and the spiritual to release your destiny' Dr Rennie Du Plessis
https://www.amazon.co.uk/dp/B07Z787J3H

4.'Create your New Mind: Solve the mind puzzle and create the best version on you' Dr Rennie Du Plessis
https://www.amazon.co.uk/dp/B07Y5WC9GW

5.'Gifts for Destiny and Life' Rennie Du Plessis and A Victor https://www.amazon.co.uk/dp/B08CHLMPWN

6.'Why we believe what we Believe: Uncovering our biological need for meaning, spirituality, and truth' Andrew Newberg and Mark Robert Waldman
https://www.amazon.co.uk/Why-Believe-What-Uncovering-Spirituality/dp/0743274970/

7.'The Little Book on Church Counselling: Creating a safe place to bring wholeness and healing.' Dr Rennie Du Plessis
https://www.amazon.co.uk/dp/1999720571

8.Positive affect and biological function in everyday life.
https://www.sciencedirect.com/science/article/abs/pii/S0197458005002769

9.Depressed mood, positive affect, and heart rate variability in patients with suspected coronary artery disease.
https://pubmed.ncbi.nlm.nih.gov/18941130/

10.Nova Scotia health survey.
https://www.ncbi.nlm.nih.gov/pmc/articles/PMC2862179/

11.Emotional style and susceptibility to the common cold.
https://pubmed.ncbi.nlm.nih.gov/12883117/

12.Trait positive affect and antibody response to hepatitis B vaccination.
https://www.sciencedirect.com/science/article/abs/pii/S088915910500139X

13.Evidence that secretory IgA antibody is associated with daily mood.
https://pubmed.ncbi.nlm.nih.gov/3585705/

14.Are Happy People Healthier?
https://www.sciencedirect.com/science/article/abs/pii/S009265660192327X

15. Positive Emotions in early life and longevity.
https://www.apa.org/pubs/journals/releases/psp805804.pdf

16.Change your walking style, change your mood.
https://www.sciencedaily.com/releases/2014/10/141015143259.htm

17.Smile Therapy.
https://www.psychologytoday.com/gb/blog/isnt-what-i-expected/201208/try-some-smile-therapy

18. Grin and Bear It: The Influence of Manipulated Facial Expression on the Stress Response.
https://journals.sagepub.com/doi/abs/10.1177/095679797612445312

19.Take a Stand.
https://www.nytimes.com/2014/09/21/fashion/amy-cuddy-takes-a-stand-TED-talk.html

20.Stress relief from laughter? It's no joke.
https://www.mayoclinic.org/healthy-lifestyle/stress-management/in-depth/art-20044456?pg=1

21.How the simple act of savouring can make you happier.
https://my.happify.com/hd/savoring-makes-us-happier-infographic/

22.The science behind gratitude.
https://my.happify.com/hd/the-science-behind-gratitude/

23.Boost self-esteem.
https://my.happify.com/hd/how-to-boost-self-esteem-and-overcome-imposter-syndrome/?fbclid=IwAR2eHbdnofGFpyZwHO4ZuV-KbLYJ9TsJvhkDbantZG8UQQ9QH7aejYshSaw

24.The science of giving: why giving is good for you.

https://my.happify.com/hd/science-of-giving-infographic/

25.How empathy can change your life.
https://my.happify.com/hd/empathy-can-change-your-life-infographic/

Printed in Great Britain
by Amazon

54245661R00163